Books by Dr. Joyce Brothers

WIDOWED

THE SUCCESSFUL WOMAN: HOW YOU CAN HAVE A
CAREER, A HUSBAND AND A FAMILY—AND NOT FEEL
GUILTY ABOUT IT

WHAT EVERY WOMAN OUGHT TO KNOW ABOUT LOVE
AND MARRIAGE

WHAT EVERY WOMAN SHOULD KNOW ABOUT MEN

HOW TO GET WHATEVER YOU WANT OUT OF LIFE

BETTER THAN EVER

THE BROTHERS SYSTEM FOR LIBERATED
LOVE AND MARRIAGE

WOMAN

TEN DAYS TO A SUCCESSFUL MEMORY

WIDOWED

Dr. Joyce Brothers

Simon and Schuster
New York   London   Toronto   Sydney   Tokyo   Singapore

Simon and Schuster
Simon & Schuster Building
Rockefeller Center
1230 Avenue of the Americas
New York, New York 10020

Designed by Nina D'Amario/Levavi & Levavi
Manufactured in the United States of America

1   3   5   7   9   10   8   6   4   2

Library of Congress Cataloging in Publication Data

Brothers, Joyce.
Widowed/Joyce Brothers
p. cm.
1. Widows—United States—Psychology. 2. Loss
(Psychology) 3. Widows—United States—Biog-
raphy. 4. Brothers, Joyce. I. Title.
HQ1058.5.U5B76   1990
306.88—dc20   90-10174
                                                          CIP

ISBN 0-671-55266-X

I dedicate this book to every woman and every man who has lost a dearly beloved person— whether to death of the body or death of love. I hope my chronicle of how I weathered the storms of grief may give you hope and courage.

WIDOWED

Introduction

❧

There came a midnight only weeks after Milt's death when I was driving home from somewhere. The thought of returning to the empty apartment was more than I could face. Why go home? There was no one there. No one to care. There was no point in going on. There was no point to anything anymore.

I was driving Milt's red Porsche. It was pitch black out, just my headlights thrusting through the night. The highway was deserted. Why not end it all? Crash into a tree? They would think I had simply lost control of the car. My suffering would be over.

It was a ten-second temptation. I learned in those few seconds that I could never give up on life, no matter how lonely and sad and tired of it I was. Whatever life held for me, I had to face it. Loneliness and all.

I drove home slowly, tears streaming down my face.

PART
1

~~~

FROM WIFE TO WIDOW

One

Six years ago I devised an exercise I called "the widow game" to help Trudy, a woman I had known for several years. Trudy complained that her husband was so unutterably dull that she was considering divorce or, at the very least, taking a lover. She spent hours fantasizing how great life would be without him. It was a classic case of what is commonly termed the "seven-year itch," which afflicts women as well as men.

Despite her complaints, I felt the marriage could be revitalized. "Before you do or say anything irrevocable," I told her, "I want you to try a psychological exercise. I think it will teach you something about yourself that will surprise you. I call it 'the widow game.' I want you to pretend that your husband is dead."

She rolled her eyes. She shrugged. She sighed. But she agreed.

"As of this minute you are a widow," I instructed her, "and you are going to be a widow for the next seven days. When you wake up tomorrow, pretend that he is not lying there beside you. You have no one to talk to. You drink your coffee alone. In the course of the day, you are to do all the things you usually depend on him to do. Take out the garbage. Put up a curtain rod. Call the garage to complain about the bill for tuning up the car. Bring in the logs for the fireplace. Stop by the liquor store on your way home from work. Whatever.

"If it is something that you cannot cope with by yourself, then pretend that you have to find someone to do it for you. As nearly as you can, lead the life you would lead if he were not there.

"If he does not feel like having sex one night, imagine what it would be like not to have sex with him ever again. If you wake up in the middle of the night and feel comforted just to have him there beside you, think how you will feel all those nights when you wake up and there is no one there.

"If he pays you a compliment or thanks you for something or gives you a present, think how it is going to be without his thoughtfulness and appreciation the rest of your life. If he tells you something interesting that went on at work or a joke that he heard, think how it is going to be without his sharing his life with you.

"Don't cheat by telling yourself that if he were not in your life, there would be someone else, someone more stimulating, more attractive, sexier. Chances are that there would not be. Remember that without him, you will join the ranks of the 7.3 million unmarried women. According to the last census, there are 7.3 million more marriageable women than men. Even if you should manage to find another man, you could not be sure he would be a better husband.

"When the week is over," I told her, "let yourself rejoice that you are not a widow, that he is still there beside you sharing your life. Be grateful for all those things you don't have to do by yourself."

Trudy called me at the end of the week. "You were right," she said. "Life without him would be terrible. He brought me coffee in bed Sunday morning, the way he always does, and I burst into tears. I was thinking that no one would ever love me enough to bring me coffee in bed again. He couldn't figure out what hit me. I told him I was crying because I was so happy."

"The widow game" had been a success. I was happy for Trudy, and I was so pleased that the psychological exercise I had devised worked so well that I included it in my book, *What Every Woman Ought to Know About Love and Marriage.*

I never dreamed that five short years later I would be a widow myself, one of those leftover women. For me, it was no game. It was cruel reality, much worse than anything I could have imagined.

When my husband died after an eighteen-month battle with cancer, I thought my life was over. There was nothing I wanted to live for. I was full of tears and self-pity. I felt lost and frightened and lonely. I was angry, self-centered, and, in my preoccupation with my grief, I fear I was boring. The truth is that by and large, no matter how calm and controlled and accepting a face she may present to the world, a new widow is miserable and can be a very difficult creature.

What else could she be? The most important person in her life is no longer there. She has lost the love and companionship of the person with whom she has shared much of her life. She has lost status, both social and economic. She has lost her future. She cannot believe what has happened to her. Cannot accept it. "Why me?" she asks over and over again. And there is no answer.

I have always thought of myself as a teacher, sharing my knowledge of psychology through the media, but in the winter of 1989 after Milt died, I became a student again. My subjects were the grim ones—dying and death, fear and grief and loneliness—all subjects that I had written and spoken about hundreds of times; but suddenly they were new to me. No matter how much research you have done, when a whole chunk is torn out of your life, when

forty-two years of love and sharing go down the drain
(we were engaged for three years and married for
thirty-nine), you face the unknown, terra incognita,
and it is frightening.

I cannot promise a widow that what I have to say
in this book will blunt her raw sense of loss or banish
her loneliness. What I can do is chart the course of
the pain—horrendous, unceasing, and cruel—that
we call grief and reassure her that this is normal and
that all widows travel this same road. And I can offer
hope.

The pain is necessary. Only by experiencing it to
its full degree can you heal yourself. When Milt died
I found myself in a dark tunnel of grief. There was
only the past (and I could not go back) and the present
(a cold and lonely hell). I could not envision a future.
There was no light at the end of the tunnel.

I spent the first six or seven months after he died
in one long wail of despair. What was to become of
me? What was I to do? What was left in life for me?
For one mad moment I hovered on the brink of sui-
cide. Overnight I found myself in a world that I had
never imagined, a world that had no logic, no sta-
bility.

I was more fortunate than many women. I had no
young children dependent on me. I was financially
comfortable. I had my work. But work, although it
provided a discipline and a framework for my days,
offered no escape from my misery.

I maintained my lecture schedule, made television

appearances, wrote my columns, flew back and forth across the country, but it was all on automatic. The zest was gone. There was no one to share my triumphs and disappointments. When I came home at night and stood outside the empty apartment scrabbling through my purse for the key, I would be overwhelmed by loneliness. Tears would stream down my face. I *knew* that I would never recover from my loss.

I was wrong. I have emerged from the tunnel of grief into the light. Life is better. Not the same, but good and getting better all the time. There are still tears, but they are gentler tears now. There is still the loneliness, but it is not the agonizing loneliness that gripped me last year. Best of all, I know there is a future. I have begun to get on with life, to look ahead instead of back. I find my work stimulating again.

And most of the time when I think of Milt, it is with a smile, not a tear, for he left me a blessed legacy of happy memories that I will cherish for the rest of my life.

Two

My husband was tall, trim, handsome, and a supremely healthy man. He played squash three times a week and rode his ten-speed bike (which he parked in our living room) for miles along the river. Weekends, he worked around our farm in the country, planting trees, cutting brush, digging in the garden, mowing, tapping the maple trees. When it was too cold to work outside, he worked inside on remodeling the old farmhouse, knocking down partitions, sanding the wide board floors, putting up shelves. Milt used to joke that he was the only one-armed carpenter in the country. His other arm was holding the how-to book. He had boundless energy and seemingly boundless health.

There was never anything wrong with him, beyond the occasional head cold and a minor hernia, until his early fifties, when his ophthalmologist, our daughter, Lisa, discovered in the course of a routine eye examination that he had hypertension. His internist confirmed Lisa's finding and put him on medication to lower his blood pressure. He advised Milt to stop smoking.

A few years later Milt developed a heart flutter, which scared him a little. His mother had died of a heart attack in her eighties, and so had his uncle. The flutter was serious enough for him to keep a miniaturized copy of his electrocardiogram in his wallet so that in case of emergency, a doctor would have a reading to refer to. His doctor prescribed medication for the condition and again advised him to stop smoking.

Milt smoked like a furnace, and this was a continual bone of contention between us. I could never understand why he would not stop. He was a physician. He read the medical journals. He was familiar with the studies proving that tobacco was a cause of cancer and death. Week after week he saw patients suffering from various kinds of havoc triggered by cigarettes.

After the doctor put him on medication for the heart flutter, Milt told me that this was it. He was not going to smoke anymore. But he did; he just did not smoke when I was around. There were times when I came back from an overnight lecture trip that our apartment reeked of cigarette smoke.

I knew that he had not really stopped, but I did think he had cut down. Somehow we both convinced ourselves that he was not smoking all that much and that the periods of abstinence while I was around made up for the rest of the time. At any rate, I stopped nagging. I felt that perhaps all my fussing was counterproductive and that if I just shut up, he might stop.

One of the side effects of the medication he was taking for the heart flutter was that if the dose was not calibrated precisely to the patient's needs, it caused blood to be spilled into the urine. One summer morning in 1987, a couple of days before our thirty-eighth wedding anniversary, which was July 4 (we always joked that it was such an important day that it had been declared a national holiday), Milt noticed blood in his urine and went for a checkup.

It turned out that the medication was not the cause of the blood in his urine, and he was scheduled for immediate diagnostic surgery. On July 9 he checked into Mount Sinai, where he had been on the staff almost all our married life. The surgeon performed a cystoscopy. This is major surgery. They went into the bladder to see what was causing the blood. What they found was a malignant polyp, which was categorized as Grade II, Stage A. In cancer terminology this meant that it was serious but not invasive. The cancer was confined to the inside tissue of the bladder and had not gone through the wall. They cut out the polyp, and the surgeon told us they had gotten it all. He said that Milt would have to come back every three months for checkups, but that the prognosis was good.

I didn't realize how terribly scared I had been until he said that the prognosis was good. It was like being given a second chance at life. I was still worried, but Milt was optimistic. He told me that when the cancer is caught at such an early stage, once the polyp is cut out, that usually is that. Lisa also reassured me, telling me essentially the same thing. And my secretary told me that she knew a man who had had a malignant bladder polyp removed twenty-two years ago and he was fine. So with the two physicians in the family seemingly relatively unconcerned and the knowledge that at least one man had survived twenty-two years, I tried to lower the level of my anxiety, telling myself that the odds were on our side.

Bladder cancer is the fifth most common cancer in men. It kills some 46,000 a year in the United States, and half of these cases are caused by smoking. Apart from smokers, the men who seem to be most at risk for this disease are painters, truck drivers, and drill press operators, all of whom are exposed to carcinogens in the course of their work. There are people who do *not* smoke and who are not painters or truck drivers or drill press operators who get bladder cancer, just as there are people who do not smoke who die of lung cancer, but these cases are the exceptions.

It is quite probable that if Milt had never smoked or if he had stopped smoking twenty years previously, he would never have developed bladder cancer. And he knew it. After the operation he announced that he was going to cut out smoking once and for all.

I think he tried. But there were times when his clothes smelled of smoke when he came home at night and I would ask him about it. "My patients smoke," he would say with a bit of annoyance. "There's nothing I can do about it." After his death I learned from his office nurse that he had still smoked as heavily as ever when he was at the office. Even knowing that he was putting his life at risk, he found it impossible to stop.

Heavy smokers (and those who love them) should know that there is a new urine analysis test—quantitative fluorescence image analysis—that can detect bladder cancer in many people while it is still in a very early stage, well before blood appears in the urine. Cancer cells contain larger amounts of DNA than normal cells do. These cancer cells are expelled in urine. Quantitative fluorescence image analysis uses a fluorescent dye that sticks to the DNA in the cells. Because there is more DNA in the cancer cells, these cells show up brighter when the urine is examined microscopically. This test can help save lives because if bladder cancer is detected in its earliest stages, the chances of survival are significantly greater.

Milt made an excellent recovery and had no further symptoms. It took some time for him to regain his energy, but by late summer he was able to resume his practice and we picked up the threads of our life again.

We started making plans for the future. We always tried to do special things on our vacations. When Halley's comet made its long-awaited swoop around the earth, we had taken a boat trip up the Amazon, because Milt was tremendously interested in astronomy and that was the best place to see the comet.

Now Milt suggested we go to Russia on our next vacation. So we made plans for a trip the coming spring, arranging to rent a car and drive from Moscow to Leningrad so we could see some of the countryside. And we started reading books on Russian history and art.

We also decided to go ahead with a longtime project—building a log cabin on some property we owned in Colorado. Whenever I go to a strange city to lecture or conduct a seminar, if I have a little spare time, I usually ask my hosts to show me the prettiest parts of their area. Years ago I had been shown a mountainside plot in Colorado that had one of the most spectacular views I had ever seen. When I discovered it was for sale, I decided we had to buy it. Milt thought I was crazy, but when he flew out to look at the property, he agreed that it was very special. Now we spent whole evenings working on plans for the log cabin we wanted to build there.

It was a happy time for us, happier still because of what I considered our narrow escape from disaster.

When Milt went into the hospital in October for his three-month checkup, he felt so well that neither of us was particularly concerned, although Milt was not looking forward to it. He knew what was in store for him. They do all kinds of uncomfortable examinations as well as go in for what they call a "look-see."

When I saw him in the hospital the next day, he was quite uncomfortable and full of tubes. He said the procedures had been just as painful as he had expected, but apart from grousing about the discomfort, he was in good spirits. The surgeon came in to see us late that afternoon. He said, "Everything's fine, but we won't know for sure until we get the biopsy. And that won't be until Monday."

This was a Friday. I knew there was only a skeleton staff in the lab on weekends, but I looked at that surgeon and what I saw was a very nice man stonewalling. In that instant I knew with absolute certainty that we were in terrible trouble.

I could read the surgeon's face and his posture. (This is the terrible part of being a psychologist;

25

sometimes you know too much.) This was a man who had bad news for us, but he wanted to give us a weekend reprieve.

Milt took his words at face value, and I did not share my insight with him. After visiting hours were over, I went home and called our daughter. "Lisa, we're in big trouble," I sobbed.

She was furious at me. "Mother, stop it! You keep borrowing trouble, and there's nothing wrong. It was just a polyp, and it's nothing. The surgeon told you that everything was fine. Why can't you believe him?"

Lisa had never been so angry at me. She told me that I was being ridiculous. She called me a crybaby and refused to talk to me any longer, handing the phone over to her husband, who sort of verbally patted me on the head as if I were a hysterical child and told me to stop worrying.

I was terribly hurt by Lisa's attitude. I felt more alone that night than I ever had in my whole life. It was the only time that I had ever turned to her for help, and she had rejected me.

I was a good enough psychologist to be able to read a surgeon's face and body language, but that evening I was too frightened to understand that my daughter was angry because she could not bear to hear what I was telling her. As a physician she realized that if I was right, it was bad news indeed. As a daughter she did not want to know it.

. . .

I was still crying when I went to bed. It felt so wrong to be in our bed without Milt. If ever I needed him to hold me and comfort me, this was the night. I wriggled over to his side of the bed as if that brought me closer to him, and finally I fell asleep, only to dream.

When I dream, I always know on some level that I am dreaming, and that it is not real. But this time I didn't. I dreamed that Death was in bed with me. Death was a man, a strong, burly man. I was curled up facing away from him, and he grabbed me from behind. I could feel the hair on his chest. I could feel the stubble of whiskers on his chin. I could smell his breath. And I knew that Death had me in his grasp.

I woke up with a start. My heart was pounding. I knew then in the dark middle of the night that I would be a widow.

Three

～⚬～

When I walked into Milt's room the next morning, he was sitting up. He was still in some pain, but they had told him he could go home the next day. We read the newspapers together, and Milt watched a football game while I tried to work. But I could not concentrate. That dream kept running through my head. I was cold with terror. Death truly had me in his grasp. I kept staring off into space, trying to imagine life without Milt. It was impossible.

I left reluctantly when visiting hours were over. The thought of spending another night alone in our bed had me almost paralyzed with fear. I was sure the death dream would return to haunt me. I need not have worried. I was too frightened to sleep. I was back at the hospital the minute visiting hours started, ready to take Milt home once the doctor had signed his discharge.

My joy in having him back home was poisoned by my fear of what the surgeon had to tell us—and by Milt's good spirits. He was so glad to be home. I wanted to scream at him, "Don't be so happy! Don't build up your hopes! There's nothing left to hope for!" I was sick with fear. I kept running to the bathroom. Every nerve in my body was raw. But I had to keep smiling. I only lost control once. My chin quivered and my eyes filled with tears and I fled to the kitchen to make tea and pull myself together.

Milt had absolutely no intimation of disaster. He spent the day happily watching football on television. He did not doubt for a moment but that the biopsy would confirm the surgeon's opinion that "everything was fine." I could not bear to think how he would feel when he heard what I was sure was going to be terrible news.

Monday was an agony. The doctor had told us he would call as soon as he got the results of the biopsy. I dreaded the call—and yet I could hardly wait for it. The day dragged on as I waited . . . and waited . . . and waited. I prayed that I had been wrong and that the surgeon would tell Milt he was clean as a whistle. But the longer we waited, the more certain I became that the news was bad. My sneaky little hopes that I was wrong, that I had misread the surgeon's face, that Lisa had been right about my being a hysterical crybaby, that my dream was simply a product of that hysteria, all those little hopes shriveled up and died.

I tried to maintain a normal routine and spent the day working in my office with one of my secretaries, but I could not keep from poking my head around the bedroom door every half hour and urging, "Call him. Call him."

Milt would shake his head. "Relax. He'll call when he has time," he told me patiently. "He said he'd call today, and he will."

It was after five when the call came. I rushed into the bedroom and sat on the edge of the bed. Milt was listening intently. I could tell from his face that it was the world's worst news. It was a long, long call. At one point Milt wiped a tear away with his finger. I had never seen him cry, not even when his mother died. And now, this tear trickling down his cheek . . . It tore me apart. Finally he said, "Well, thank you," and hung up.

He was silent for a moment, and then he told me that the cancer had reappeared and spread to the wall of his bladder. He was very matter-of-fact.

I stared at him. I knew the news was going to be bad, and yet it came as a shock. I could not let him know how scared I was. I threw my arms around him. "We'll beat it," I told him. "You're strong. You can beat it."

He ran his finger around my face, outlining it, and summoned up a half smile. "I'm going to do my damnedest," he promised. "I've got a lot to live for."

We held each other for a few minutes, and then Milt said, "We've got some decisions to make." The doctor had told him that there were two possibilities. He would be admitted for surgery to have his bladder removed. But before they took it out, they would do a biopsy. If the biopsy showed clean margins, they would go ahead and take out the bladder; if it showed that the cancer had spread outside the bladder, they would simply sew him up again and leave him to live as long as he could.

If they took out the bladder, he would have to have an ostomy bag to collect the urine. There were two options. One was to install an internal duct that went through his penis so he would not have to have an outside bag. The other was to have an outside bag.

We discussed both procedures during the next few days with several physicians. We learned that the potential medical consequences, especially the possibility of infection, were far greater with the internal duct. When it came to making the decision, neither of us had to think twice. The outside bag was definitely the best bet.

We also learned that with either procedure, Milt would almost surely be impotent, since they would do a prostatectomy as well as the radical cystectomy. I told Milt it made no difference at all to me. Sex was a very minor consideration in this context. Life itself was all that mattered now.

It seems strange, but I cannot even remember the last time we made love—when it was or anything about it. If you don't know that it is the last time you will ever make love, well, after thirty-nine years of marriage, sex tends to be a familiar pleasure that you take for granted. All I know is that our last lovemaking was sometime before the polyp was removed on July 9. The surgery had left him extremely weak and uncomfortable, and while he made a good recovery, he seemed to have lost his sexual drive. I like to think that it was on July 4, our wedding anniversary.

Once we had decided on the outside ostomy bag, the surgery was scheduled almost immediately. A radical cystectomy—taking out a bladder—is a complicated and risky piece of surgery, an eight-hour operation. They let me stay with him in the holding room outside the operating room until he was wheeled in. I stood there that October morning holding his hand and trying to smile until they came for him. Then I went back to his room and waited.

An hour later there was a knock on the door and Dr. Weber walked in. When I saw him I came as close to having a heart attack as I ever have in my life. My heart just stopped. It clamped down and stopped. It was an eight-hour operation. What was the surgeon doing here?

Actually he had come as an act of kindness. Just as Milt had been wheeled into the operating room, an emergency patient had been rushed in. It was a matter of life and death, so Milt's surgery had to be postponed for a couple of hours. Weber wanted to let me know that they had not even started, so that I would not worry later on.

He came back in the early evening and told me everything was fine. The margins had been clean. They had taken out the bladder. Milt was doing well. The surgeon was obviously and openly pleased. It was wonderful news. We were still going to have a life together.

Milt never smoked again after this operation. It took a scare of this magnitude to make him stop. What was interesting was that as soon as he stopped smoking, the heart flutter he had had for some five or six years went away. He was too embarrassed to tell any of his doctors that the reason the flutter went away was because he had finally stopped smoking.

I could not help thinking, If you had only stopped ten years ago, twenty years ago, thirty years ago, none of this would have happened. I was angry. How could he have been so stupid! How could he have done this to himself! To me! If he had only given up cigarettes earlier, he would not have had to have this operation. I am still angry about this.

Angry as I was, I never mentioned his smoking again, never brought it up. I knew that if I did, it would be what we used to call a "Bunny, I sez." This was one of those phrases couples develop over the years. When we were engaged, Milt used to call me

33

Bunny or Bunnynose, and I called him Rabbit. (You must remember that we were very young.)

There came a day after we were married when I wanted to do something. I can't even remember what it was. Milt said I'd be sorry if I did it, but I went ahead anyway. He was right. I was sorry. And Milt said, quite tenderly, "Bunny, I sez it would never work out." The phrase struck us as very brilliant. It became our way of telling each other "I told you so."

How could I ever have said—even though it was true—"Bunny, I sez if you did not stop smoking, you'd be sorry."

I know now that both Milt and I underestimated how strongly addictive nicotine is. It is physically, psychologically, and socially addictive. According to the most recent research, approximately half the people who make a real effort to stop smoking do not succeed. After a week, a month, a year, they resume smoking. The majority never try to stop again.

The best thing a person who really wants to stop smoking can do is to get professional help, someone or some program that will not only help him or her stop smoking, but will also help that person remain a nonsmoker. Many family physicians are learning to treat smoking as the addiction it is instead of just a bad habit. The emphasis is less on simply stopping and more on remaining a nonsmoker day after day, week after week, month after month. Every day that a smoker does not smoke is a triumph. It takes years for the addiction to disappear, and for some people the craving never disappears and they have to fight the addiction day by day to the end of their lives.

I feel guilty that I did not give Milt more positive reinforcement each and every day that I knew he did not smoke. My attitude was always, "Wonderful! I'm so happy you're stopping!" It was not enough.

I have learned, however, that there is one thing that can turn a nicotine addict into a nonsmoker overnight. And that is fear, the fear that hits you in the gut when you suddenly and finally realize that smoking is fatal, that you are killing yourself. Milt stopped when his cancer spread. Two of my secretaries who were heavy smokers stopped at the same time. They got the message, and so far neither of them has resumed smoking.

As soon as he was well enough, they taught him how to take care of the ostomy and change the bag and all that. I wanted to learn how, but Milt said he did not want me to have anything to do with it, so I just stayed in the room and listened while the nurse instructed him.

I had a secret fear that the first time I saw Milt naked after the operation I might be upset by the ostomy. This really worried me. I could take the scars that crisscrossed his belly in my stride. But a hole? Was I a good enough actress to hide my dismay, even horror? I was ashamed of feeling this way, but

I was truly full of dread. As it turned out, there was never anything about it that was a turnoff to me. There was no odor. Nothing. It never bothered me in the least, not even the first time I saw it.

Nor did it limit Milt's activities. He could walk. He could drive. He could fly. When we drove to the country on weekends, we would have to stop once so he could empty the bag, but that was no problem. We did everything we had done before, except make love. And that was a small price to pay for a man's life. Everything was fine, could not have been better given the circumstances. We told ourselves we were going to beat the odds.

We—the physician and the psychologist—were now heavily into denial. As a physician, Milt knew that the prognosis for bladder cancer, once it has spread through the wall of the bladder, was very grave, but he never discussed this fact. As a psychologist, I knew all about denial. But I did not deny. Oh, no! I called my denial hope. I knew Milt was deathly ill. My head knew it. My whole body knew it. I knew I would be a widow. But I fought this knowledge almost until the day he died.

Actually, at that point it was hard to believe what we knew deep down inside, no matter how much we denied it. Milt had made a good recovery from surgery. He was getting stronger every day. He had gone back to work and was seeing patients. It did seem as if there was reason for hope.

Four

Milt had his three-month postsur-
gery checkup on January 9. Everything looked good.
And then, ten days later, from one day to the next,
he developed a problem. He complained of a pain in
his abdomen, and his bowel movements were not
normal. He described them as consisting of little
"wood shavings."

So it was back to the hospital for another examination. The doctors were concerned that the cancer
might have spread to the bowel. (In fact it had, but
it was months before they found it.) He was examined by the urologist. And the gastroenterologist.
And the proctologist. Milt described it as being gang-
raped. There was an endless series of invasive prob-
ings plus a CAT scan, which he hated. For him to

stay absolutely still during that long twenty minutes while he was being scanned was close to torture. After putting him through all this, they found nothing and sent him home.

The bowel symptoms got worse and worse. He developed a pain in his midsection and started running a fever. He went into the hospital again. They put him through all the tests again and found nothing. Finally, after two weeks in the hospital, they biopsied his liver and found that the cancer had spread to his liver.

It was the worst news ever. When the doctor told me, I almost vomited. It was so unfair! Everything had seemed to be going so well, and now this.

Milt's oncologist, Dr. Martin Weiner, started him on chemotherapy. A new formulation of medications called M-VAC (an acronym for its main components, methotrexate, Velban, Adriamycin, and cisplatinum) had just become available. This was the first chemotherapy that had any real effect on the liver. M-VAC was not being used at Mount Sinai, but it was used by Dr. Alan Yagoda at Memorial Sloan-Kettering Cancer Center just a couple of miles away. Lisa had heard of it, and she persuaded Dr. Weiner to call in Dr. Yagoda as a consult on Milt's case.

According to the statistics, Milt had only a few weeks left to live. But Dr. Yagoda radiated confidence and told us he thought that he could get Milt normal again.

The side effects of the chemotherapy were horrendous. They had to give him medication to keep him from throwing up. He was deathly tired and weak as a kitten most of the time. His hair fell out. But Dr. Yagoda's optimism was justified. Instead of having only a few weeks more to live, Milt had nearly a year.

One of the debilitating side effects of the chemotherapy was hiccups that went on and on and totally exhausted him. I had studied hypnosis and was able to stop his hiccups by rubbing and stimulating an area in the diaphragm. This gentle massage gave him so much comfort that it became part of our daily routine. I would sit beside him for hours on end—just rubbing his tummy.

Another thing I did was brush his hair. I bought a soft baby hairbrush, a little blue hairbrush, and I used to brush what was left of his hair. He grumbled that I was babying him, but he loved it. And I loved doing it. I could not make him better, but I could make his time a little better, a little easier.

These were the peaceful hours when we were together and he could relax and I could feel that I was helping him a little. We were so close at these times. I used to feel overwhelmed by my love for him.

He was in and out of the hospital so often that when I try to think back now, it is all a blur. One hospital visit is so much like the one before and the one after. The bowel problem never seemed to improve; he was in constant pain. At one point we went to Baltimore to see a physician at Johns Hopkins who had developed a special diagnostic series. He did a complete bowel workup, but, like the others, he found nothing.

Milt's bowel obstructed twice, and each time I had to rush him to the hospital so they could go in and take care of the obstruction. It happened once when our nine-year-old grandson, Micah, was visiting. I could not leave Micah alone in the apartment, so I woke him up at five o'clock in the morning and took him to the emergency room with us. They had to operate on Milt to remove the obstruction, so I took Micah for a walk. It seemed unreal to be walking along Fifth Avenue across from Central Park at that hour of the morning, waiting for Milt to come out of surgery.

This particular bowel obstruction episode turned out to have a silver lining. As I said, they had to operate to deal with it, and since they were inside, they took a biopsy of the liver. It showed that the liver was totally clear of cancer!

The surgeon could not believe it. He was sure there had been a mistake, and he went down to the lab and rechecked the slides himself. It was no mistake. It was true. The liver was normal in size and free of cancer. Our hopes rose again, although Milt still suffered agonies from his bowel symptoms and was terribly weak.

. . .

Milt closed his office that spring. He was just too weak and tired to carry on his practice. He sent out thousands of letters to patients, past and present, to let them know he was giving up the practice, and he got hundreds of letters and calls in return, which cheered him immensely. I don't think he had realized before quite how much his patients liked him and how very important he was to them.

It made him more determined than ever to find just the right man or woman to take over his practice. He ended up by selling it for much less than its book value. This was typical of Milt. A saleswoman who examined Milt's books preparatory to putting the practice on the market told me, "In all my years in this business I have never seen a doctor who carried so many people on the books." Milt never charged a rabbi. Never charged a rabbinical student. Never charged another doctor. Never charged a doctor's wife. Or child. Never charged a relative. Never charged a relative of a relative. So why should he sell his practice for what it was worth?

Milt's had been a very special practice. The office had always been full of laughter. He took medicine seriously, but he liked to have fun. One of his patients, a radio announcer, had recorded an emergency alert for an oncoming blizzard for him. Milt always had music from a radio station piped into the waiting room, and on the hottest day of summer he would play the emergency alert about the oncoming blizzard and the patients in the waiting room would stiffen as if they were not sure what they'd heard. Every once in a while a patient would scurry out, presumably to get ready for the approaching blizzard. Every Friday he held a "medical conference" at the end of office hours. That's what he called it, but it was really a wine and cheese party for his nurses and any patients who were there at the end of the day.

And he made terrible jokes. There is a test for colon cancer where you take a smear of your bowel movement and put it on a card and send it to the lab. Milt would tell his patients just what to do, and then he would add, "Be sure to send it turd-class mail." There were many others of the same caliber. His patients relaxed in the informal atmosphere— all except one, a television producer, who never came back after his first visit, saying, "I don't need a Marx brother for a doctor."

Milt ended up selling the practice to a physician he knew and respected, a man he felt sure would take good care of his patients. He had a chance to sell the practice for three times as much, but he felt the man was just not good enough. "I'm not going to spend a lifetime devoting myself to my patients," he said, "and then sell them down the river."

I had to sell Milt's office after he died, and it was one of the hardest things I have ever done in my life. I did not want to sell it. I even considered giving up the apartment and moving into the office, which would have been ridiculous.

During the final negotiations between the buyer and the lawyer who was handling it for me (his wife had been Milt's office nurse, and they had known us for years and years), the prospective buyer came to take a last look around before signing the papers. The three of us were walking through the office, and the lawyer said, "There's nothing special about this office, except that the walls are filled with laughter."

After Milt sold his practice, he was mostly at home. He read and slept and watched sports programs on television. I used to sit beside him to keep him company. I would read my professional journals, cut out articles that I wanted to save, answer my mail—and sometimes I just sat there and held his hand.

Almost the only times he got dressed and went out were when he had to go for chemotherapy or check into the hospital for tests and more surgery. But once in a while I was able to coax him into getting dressed and going out with me for some fresh air. He used to grumble and say my faith in fresh air was unfounded, but I felt that when he stayed in the house all the time, night and day would get confused and he would not sleep well. Once I got him outside, he usually enjoyed our little walks.

One summer evening we bought a pizza and sat in the park and ate it. That was a triumph in itself since he had lost his appetite almost completely. I used to cook all the things he liked, but most of the time he just picked at whatever was on his plate.

Some days we just walked for a block or two, sometimes three or four if he was feeling strong. We used to speculate about the people who lived in the houses we passed. I always tried to have a destination—the bakery or the spot where there was a wonderful river view or the toy store, where we would pick up something for one of our grandchildren.

One October day when I was taping a television show, he went out by himself. It was my birthday, and he wanted to get me a present. He knew I liked amusing pieces of china and ceramics. I have cookie jars that look like houses and breakfast plates shaped like chickens, all sorts of things like that.

The present he found was a ceramic apple with a little worm on the cover. We have our own apples at the farm, and we used to tell ourselves that we made the world's best applesauce. I can't express just how much that present meant to me. It seemed like a promise that he would be around to enjoy that applesauce with me.

And he was—but just once. He seemed to be feeling stronger that October, and one sunny morning I drove him up to our farm. We had our ritual weekend breakfast, only this day it was lunch. We stopped to buy eggs from the woman down the road who keeps her own chickens—absolutely fresh eggs, a different food from the supermarket egg.

Milt made the eggs. Fried eggs were his culinary

specialty. He had a frying pan dedicated to eggs. I was not allowed to use it for anything. He never even let me wash it but used to wipe it out himself when he finished cooking.

And he made the coffee. He ground his own special blend of coffee beans and brewed it in his special coffeemaker. It was wonderful coffee. I always used to say that if he were ever to leave me for a younger woman, I would insist on coming over every morning for coffee.

I made the toast and squeezed the orange juice and put our own applesauce into my birthday apple. I was thrilled because he ate everything. He had not eaten that much for weeks.

After breakfast he went upstairs alone and looked around. Each bedroom represented long weekends of hard work. Over the years we had scraped and painted until each room was fresh and welcoming, just as country bedrooms should be.

Then he went outside. I watched him stand looking at the meadow where Lisa had been married twelve years ago. I watched as he walked down to the brook where he and Micah used to fish. Finally he came in, absolutely white with fatigue but happy.

He rested for a while, and then we started back to the city. The last thing he said, as he was locking the door behind us, was, "It's so beautiful here." There was a wistful note in his voice. We both knew he would probably never see the farm again. And he never did.

Five

We never talked about death. Our conversations were full of "when I get back on my feet," "as soon as you get your strength back," "once I finish this chemotherapy series," "next spring, we have to put a new roof on the barn . . ." We always kept the future open. One day life would be wonderful again. Was it bravery? Or self-delusion? Whom were we trying to fool? I don't know. All I knew was that death was an unspeakable word, a taboo subject.

The past, like the future, was safe. Reminiscence was a pleasure and a comfort. "Remember when . . ." Milt would say, and we would be off in the wonderful past. Our first kiss . . . the first time I met his mother . . . the day we went to the races and won . . . our second honeymoon . . . our first honeymoon. We had a lifetime of memories. And I clutched every one of them to my heart.

Milt and I met one summer at Sackman's, a family farm resort in the Catskills where my family had always vacationed. I was still a teenager and he was twenty, and we knew immediately that we were meant for each other.

We were inseparable for the five days he was there. We went for long walks. We went rowing on the lake. We did a lot of kissing and cuddling in the hayloft. And we talked endlessly. We were amazed at how much we had in common. I had grown up on Long Island and in Manhattan; he had grown up in Queens. Both our families had vacationed at Sackman's, but never at the same time.

Milt was fresh from three years in the navy, where he had been attached to a marine corps medical unit. Now that the war was over—our war was World War II—he was about to start his sophomore year at Cornell, where I was a junior. His work as a medic had convinced him that medicine was his future, and he planned to go to medical school after graduation. I planned to go to graduate school at Columbia to work for a master's and then a doctorate in psychology, which would prepare me to teach.

We saw a lot of each other at Cornell that fall, and we got pinned shortly before Christmas and engaged when I graduated from Cornell. We got married when Milt graduated a year later.

47

I would have done anything for Milt, but one thing I tried just did not work out. I was a virgin when we married. For some reason—perhaps because I had read too many trashy romantic novels and he had overheard too many old wives' tales at home—both Milt and I believed that losing her virginity was very painful for a woman. This did not really bother me. I figured millions of women had survived the pain, but Milt said that he was afraid he might hurt me on our wedding night.

I did not want him to be worried about anything on our wedding night. So I, a very intellectual young woman, decided on what I considered a logical solution. I went to a gynecologist to have my hymen stretched. It was a miserable, dreadful experience! There I was on an examining table with my feet in the stirrups for the first time in my life and a strange doctor peering between my legs. He inserted a small disk and told me that each time I came back, he would insert a larger one. Well, it was so horrid and unromantic that I never went back. Fortunately, as any woman knows, losing one's virginity is no big deal.

And our honeymoon was blissful—except for the last night, when we had our first fight. Milt had taken a long shower and used up all the hot water, leaving none for me. If I had known the term *male chauvinist pig* then, I certainly would have used it.

We made up and promised each other we would never fight again. But of course we did—all through our marriage. We squabbled over a hundred things. I thought he was too strict with Lisa; he thought I was too lenient. He would want to buy something; I would say it was too expensive—and anyway we didn't need it. He thought roast beef should be well done; I thought it should be rare. None of our fights was serious. We boiled up and simmered down.

We lived with my folks after we got married. Not until Milt got his medical degree and started his internship at Mount Sinai in New York City were we able to afford an apartment of our own. By that time I was working for my doctorate and teaching psychology at Hunter College and Columbia.

The apartment was a dump, but we painted it and thought it wonderful. It was a very happy time. The future was boundless. My husband, the doctor, and I, the Ph.D. And a baby on the way. The sky was the limit. Together we thought we could do anything. And, for the most part, we were able to do almost everything we wanted. Not everything. We had wanted three or four children, but after Lisa was born, I was deathly ill with acute septicemia, which put an end to that dream. But we had Lisa, and she was the joy of our lives.

Our only problem was that we were poor. We were just managing to scrape by, but even so I stopped working when Lisa was born. Milt's pay as an intern was pitiful, but we decided that somehow we would manage. Nothing was more important than giving our child the best possible start in life, and I believed that meant my staying home with her, at least until she was three.

Making it work was harder than we had expected. Television was our only entertainment during those lean days. We always watched *The $64,000* Question, the first of the big TV quiz shows. Everybody watched it on Tuesday nights.

One night I said, "I could do that."

"So could I," said Milt. "Why don't we?"

We joked about it a little, and then we became serious. Why not try? We decided that I should do it, because I had more time on my hands. Milt worked seventy and eighty hours a week at the hospital.

I analyzed the characteristics of the people they chose as contestants. They all had one thing in common: they presented a paradox—a shoe repairman was an expert on opera, a tough marine was a gourmet cook, and so on. There was nothing unusual about me. So I cast about for occupations or areas of knowledge that would seem incongruous for a young woman. I narrowed down the choices to plumbing and boxing. Milt turned thumbs down on plumbing. "Who wants to hear about frozen pipes and blocked toilets?"

And so it was boxing. Looking back, I have to admire our audacity in believing that I could learn enough about the manly art of boxing to get on the show, but one thing we did not lack was self-confidence.

It was a joint endeavor from the very start. We rented films of boxing matches and a projector, and we watched the films over and over again. We worked together every step of the way. My mother took care of Lisa for me, and I did nothing but study. I got up at six in the morning and studied until one the next morning. I memorized thousands of statistics. Milt would come home from the hospital and throw questions about boxing at me until he was exhausted and I was numb. It was total immersion. But I had an important goal, so it was easy to do. When you are young, and terribly motivated, you learn very easily when you want to.

When we thought I was ready, I wrote the producer of the show outlining my qualifications to be a contestant. After an interview, I was accepted. What happened then was incredible. I was on week after week after week. I kept winning. Then one night it was all over. I won the $64,000!

That was an awful lot of money in the 1950s. It was like winning a million today. That money changed our lives in many ways, all of them good. It gave us both a chance to establish ourselves in our professions. It was enough so that Milt was able to buy and furnish an office and establish his own New York practice instead of having to wait years and years, enough for us to move to a larger apartment, enough for us to buy a car.

Besides the money, winning turned me into an overnight celebrity and opened the door to a career somewhat different from the one I had envisioned for myself. There were dozens of requests for me to appear here and there, to lecture on this and that. It turned out that people were far more interested in psychology and what it meant in their daily lives than they were in boxing. Eventually there was a radio show, a column, a book. More and more doors kept opening.

Milt's career kept pace. An internist with a specialty in endocrinology and a subspecialty in diabetes, he was highly respected in his field. He was also an associate professor at Mount Sinai. He loved to teach, and on more than one occasion the medical students at Mount Sinai voted him their best teacher. We often told each other how fortunate we were that both of us had work that made us happy.

We kept our working lives separate, but we were always there for each other. If I were to say, "I really need you to come with me to this dinner at the New Zealand embassy in Washington," or, "I've been asked to appear on a husband-and-wife television show. Would you come? It's important to me," he would always be there for me.

And when he asked me to address the Juvenile Diabetes Association, I was happy to talk about how to deal with a child who has a chronic illness. When he was named Man of the Year by the New York YMCA, I rushed back from California so that I could introduce him at the ceremony.

At home, however, my career and his profession were put aside. There we were husband and wife, mom and dad. We could have been any American family, except that our lives were probably quieter than most.

Our lives really revolved around Lisa. We used to move heaven and earth to make time to attend Parents' Day and all the school plays and functions. We shared our lives with her as much as possible. Milt used to take her to the hospital and to his office. I would take her to a radio station or television studio when there was something especially interesting going on.

Once (and this became a favorite family story) I took her out of school for a week to go on a cross-country speaking tour with me. I wanted her to know what my life away from home was like. I also thought it would be educational.

On the plane coming home, I asked her what she had learned from our trip. She pondered a minute and then said, "I learned you should not take your shoes off when you sit at the head table because people can see your feet." So much for the broadening influence of travel.

When Lisa went off to college, our home lives became even quieter. Our idea of a wonderful evening was to sit around in our robes and read or just talk. We were usually in bed by nine, and we would watch a little television before we turned off the light. We were both early risers since Milt left shortly before six most mornings to make his hospital rounds, and I always got up to make breakfast for him.

We loved to work together at the farm. We spent hours in the kitchen making ketchup from our own tomatoes and applesauce from our own apples. One year we decided to learn how to tap our maple trees for sap and make our own maple syrup. This was so much fun that Milt decided we needed more maple trees, so we ordered fifty and planted our own maple bush. It was hard work, but we enjoyed every minute of it.

Our Saturday nights at the farm were special. We always bought a lottery ticket on the way up there, and our entertainment for the night was getting into bed and watching the ten o'clock news to see if we had won. We never did, but we never lost hope.

Perhaps the happiest day of our lives was the April day we danced at Lisa's wedding. Just as Milt and I knew the moment we met that we were meant for each other, we knew the moment *they* met that Lisa and Amir were meant for each other. They dated for a while, and then they drifted apart. Then when she was in medical school at Tulane in New Orleans and he was in medical school at Baylor in Houston, they got together again. And this time they realized what Milt and I had known all along.

They were married in the great meadow behind our old farmhouse, where we set up a huge tent with a dance floor. When Milt and I followed Lisa and

Amir out onto the dance floor, I was so happy there were tears in my eyes.

It was like the closing of one chapter in our lives and the beginning of another. A chapter, I thought, that would be even happier than all that had gone before, because Milt and I were even more in love with each other than we had been the day we married.

I never thought our love story would end. Each new grandchild was a blessing that made our lives richer. We had so many plans. And now? Now everything was in the lap of the gods.

One day life is golden. The next day, without even knowing it, you turn a corner, and from that time on the light gradually dims until you find yourself all alone in the dark of loss and grief. You look back and realize, Yes, that is when it started.

Six

❦

Nothing got better. Everything got worse. One could almost measure the progress of Milt's illness by his hospital visitors. Many, many doctors came by in the beginning when there was real hope that he would recover. It was like a little party most afternoons. But as he got sicker and sicker, and was in and out of the hospital all the time, there was a gradual withdrawal by these visitors. Most doctors have a hard time coping with death. Dedicated to healing, they see death as an unsuccessful outcome, a personal defeat, and coping with the death of a colleague is especially difficult because it makes them face their own mortality. By the end, only the doctors who were treating Milt and a few old friends came by.

When the cancer spread to his bones, they started Milt on another course of chemotherapy. Each time they discovered the cancer had spread, it was a catastrophe. There would be all these painful and wearying tests and then the nervous waiting for the results. They gave him some really heavy drugs in addition to his other medication because of the almost unbearable pain from the bone cancer.

Then, over Thanksgiving weekend, Milt went crazy. Literally. It was a four-day weekend, and no doctors were around. I left messages, but no one called back. By Sunday morning Milt was really out of his head—raving mad. I was frantic.

When on Monday I still could not get hold of any of his doctors, I called my son-in-law, who—like my daughter—is an ophthalmologist.

"Amir," I told him, "we're in big trouble. Milt is out of his mind, and I can't get hold of anyone. I think all the drugs he has been taking for pain have driven him crazy."

Amir said he would call an oncologist friend of his and ask him if he could go anywhere in the world for relief from cancer pain, where he would go. He called back within the hour and gave me two names. He said he thought Dr. Kathleen Foley, head of the Pain Clinic at Memorial Sloan-Kettering Cancer Center, was the better of the two.

So I called Dr. Foley. She heard the panic in my voice and said, "Bring him right in."

As I had suspected, Milt's craziness was caused by

the medication. Each of his doctors—the proctologist, the gastroenterologist, the nephrologist, and the oncologist—had prescribed the medications and painkillers they considered necessary. When we went to Johns Hopkins in Baltimore, they had prescribed more medication. I never heard anyone say, "Hey, if we give him this thing, maybe it will send him over into this kind of problem or that kind of problem."

The Pain Clinic was wonderful. They coordinated the drugs, the medications, everything, and Milt was never sent over the edge into madness by drugs again. Once they got his medications balanced, although he was never completely free of pain, he was able to live with it.

We thought Dr. Foley was great. She became important in Milt's treatment after this. Milt gave her his ultimate compliment (and you have to understand that he was an unreconstructed male chauvinist pig, but I loved him anyway). Dr. Foley had asked him a question, and he said, "You know, that's a very astute question. For a woman."

He got weaker and thinner. And crankier and angrier. I expected cranky and angry. My father had been easily angered in the months before his death, and whatever caused the flare-up, it had always been my fault. So when Milt was angry I understood this, and although it was sometimes hard to take, I did my best to ignore it.

My driving particularly incensed him. He was not strong enough to drive anymore, so I drove us back and forth to his various medical appointments, and there was just no way I could please him. It was no-win all the way. If I missed a light, he would growl, "You hit more red lights than any other human being." And no matter what route I took it was always, "Why didn't you go that way? . . . You're going too fast. . . . Why are you going so slow?" And on and on.

Anger is part of the dying process with many people. And why not? Life is sweet. Who wants it to end? I understood Milt's anger, and although it upset me, in a way I welcomed it.

Anger turned inward can eat you up alive. One of the reasons women tend to have fewer emotional problems than men is that, unlike most men, they permit themselves to cry, and this helps them get rid of their stress. If you can't get your anger out in some way—by crying or verbalizing it or by vigorous physical exercise or whatever—the stress builds up and poisons your system. It is like a thunderstorm that rumbles and rumbles and the air never gets cleared. But when you get a good clap of thunder and the lightning flashes and it starts to rain, afterward the air is clear. And that is the way it was with Milt. Once he was able to express his anger, the air was clearer, the atmosphere calmer.

I was his only target. He could not be angry at himself. He could not be angry at his doctors, because he was dependent on them. But he could be angry at me. He knew that no matter what he said or did, I would always be there for him.

Because I understood this, Milt's anger and crankiness hardly ever bothered me. If he wanted a pillow, didn't want a pillow, wanted this, wanted that, I just did what he wanted. I never snapped back at him, no matter how exasperating he was, but there were times when I could not help crying. He would push me the way a child will push his mother just to see how far he could go until I started to cry. And then he would let up.

In the beginning I used to get upset when I was out of town and called him at the hospital and asked how he felt. I knew he could not say anything positive, but it seemed uncaring if I did not ask. He always got angry and snarled, "How do you think I feel? I've got cancer and I'm in pain." I finally decided it was better to ask him even if he got angry, because it was another way of draining off his anger. Once I made myself understand this, it was easier.

I had stopped working after his surgery except for commitments that had been contracted for earlier. Whenever I had to go out of town to speak, I would plan to arrive just before I was scheduled to speak and leave as soon as possible. If there were no flights until the next day, I would charter a plane so that I did not have to be away overnight.

These efforts were for my sake more than Milt's.

I felt guilty about leaving him, but he always said, "Go on. You can't just sit around here day after day. It will do you good. Just don't stay away too long."

When I was away, either Lisa would fly from Iowa to be with her father or his sister, Margie, would fly up from Florida. Later on I would have a nurse come in and take care of him as well. I never wanted to leave him at home or in the hospital without some member of the family there. Hospitals may be full of people, but they can be the loneliest places in the world if you are ill and do not have someone near and dear with you.

People used to say that it must be a relief for me to get out of the house and have a change of atmosphere. It was anything but a relief. It was agony. My interior clock would start ticking the minute I closed the door behind me, and with each tick the level of my anxiety increased. When I got home I would be so anxious that after I got out of the elevator, I would run down the hall to our apartment. I could hardly wait to see him and be sure he was all right.

Only when I was right there on the spot did I feel secure, because I knew what was going on. Even leaving him to work in my office in the next room or go to the kitchen to cook raised my anxiety level.

I did not want to admit it to myself, but he was going steadily downhill that late fall and winter. The trip to the farm had represented one last surge of vitality. Now there were ominous signs of increasing deterioration. One that broke my heart was when he received a letter from an old friend. After reading it, he went straight to his typewriter to answer it. He wrote, "Dear Austin—Fate has not been kind to me. I have cancer."

And that is as far as he got. He was too weak to continue. He never felt up to finishing it. The letter was still in his typewriter the day he died.

Finally, during one of the hundreds of tests he was subjected to, they discovered the cause of all the bowel symptoms that had tormented him for almost a year: a malignant tumor. They started him on radiotherapy, which effectively shrank the tumor, but it was very debilitating.

It completely killed his appetite. Up to this point I was able to coax him to eat at least a few mouthfuls, but now he simply resisted. He became too weak to walk across the sidewalk from the car to the hospital. I had to push him in a wheelchair. And then it became almost all he could do to get into the wheelchair, even with my help.

He was scheduled to start another radiotherapy series for the bowel tumor the day after Christmas, but I did not think he was up to it. "He doesn't seem to be as strong as he was a week ago," I told Dr. Weiner, the oncologist.

"Let's wait another week, then," he said, "before we start the new series." Milt did not say anything, but I knew he was relieved to have even a temporary reprieve.

I thought he should be in the hospital, because they would be able to give him nourishment intravenously, and I was sure that it was his refusal to eat that was making him so weak. I suggested he ask the doctor to readmit him, but he said, "I'd rather die than go into the hospital again."

Lisa's fourth child was due the first week of January and I wanted to be with her, but I was reluctant to leave Milt while he was in this very weak state.

On the morning of Saturday, January 7, he was too weak and confused to change his ostomy bag. Since he had insisted that I have nothing to do with it, I could not help him, and no one was available on the weekend. I telephoned the hospital. I called doctors. I called nurses. No one could help me. I was on the verge of panic, but finally I just said, "Okay, I'm going to do it. I'll figure it out." And I did. I just did what seemed logical. Then when I had it all done, I discovered Milt was playing with a piece of the thing. This practically sent me into hysterics, because I couldn't figure where that piece went. It turned out to be a piece left over from another ostomy bag.

As I was fretting about trying to fit it in, Milt said, "Well, get Joyce. She'll know how to do it."

And I said, "But I *am* Joyce."

He kept saying, "Get Joyce." It almost drove me crazy. All our married life, Milt had always felt that if there was a problem, I could solve it. Now he did not even know I was there and that I *had* solved it.

The minute he dozed off and I could leave him, I called Dr. Foley. "I just don't think he's right," I told her. "He's not himself. He seems to be withdrawing. He has not been eating, and he has become increasingly confused. And now"—I started crying—"now he does not even know who I am."

"That happens," she said. "Sometimes people withdraw and don't eat well and get confused, then they come out of it themselves. And sometimes they withdraw and die. There is no way you can tell.

"He needs to be in the hospital," she told me. "I can do my best for him only if he is in the hospital. I think you should tell him that. You know, he has to decide. Does he want to live? Or does he want to die?"

I told Milt that I had talked with her. "I know how you hate to be in the hospital, but she says that it offers you your best chance of staying alive. She can do more for you in the hospital."

He did not hesitate. Not for a second. Even though he had said he would rather die than go back into the hospital again, when he had to choose, he chose life. I drove him over to Memorial immediately, and he was readmitted to the hospital.

I was still hopeful. Yes, he was weak and would not eat, but he had responded beautifully to the chemotherapy. And when they finally had found the spot in his bowel that had been bothering him all this time, and treated it with radiotherapy, they had gotten a good response. The first series had shrunk the tumor to such an extent that he was no longer having bowel problems.

Being in the hospital was demonstrably good for him. He responded almost immediately. He was taking nutrition, and within hours he was less confused.

When Amir telephoned late that afternoon to say that Lisa had just had a little girl, Milt was doing so well, I had no qualms about planning to go to Iowa and see the baby. Lisa's father-in-law said he would stay with Milt while I was away, and that put my mind completely at ease. But then Milt said, "No, don't go. I need you here."

I told him that I would not dream of going if he wanted me to stay, but then he thought about it. And after a while he said, "You know, you really should go see the baby. See her for me and give her a kiss for me."

I flew to Iowa the next morning, Sunday morning, and went straight to the hospital, where I visited with Lisa and held little Ariel. I kissed my day-old granddaughter and kissed her again for her grandfather. I stayed an hour. Lisa wanted me to stay longer. "Take a later plane," she urged, but I just did not feel easy about being away from Milt any longer. I had accomplished what I came for. I had seen Lisa and kissed the baby and assured myself that all was well with them. Mother and infant were thriving. Now all I wanted was to get back to Milt.

Visiting hours at his hospital were over by the time I got home. I was tired because I had left early that morning, and I thought, I'll go straight home to bed and see Milt in the morning. Something made me change my mind. I was not even sure they would let me up to see him after visiting hours, but I decided I would go anyway. If they won't let me see him, I thought, at least I'll feel better in my heart, because I tried.

They gave me special permission to see him. When I asked his nurse how he was doing, she said, "Just fine. He's taking nutrition. He's not confused."

That was encouraging, and I went into his room and over to the bed. I took his hand, and he opened his eyes.

"Oh, Joyce," he said. "Sit down."

He closed his eyes again, and I sat there beside him holding his hand and looking at him. My heart was bursting with conflicting emotions. I was joyful after seeing Lisa and her baby. I was sad, desperately sad. I was full of love.

I started talking. I told him about my visit with Lisa and the new baby. And I talked about our other grandchildren. How dear they all were to us. How well they were developing. I talked about Lisa and how proud we were of her and what a good mother and wife she was. I talked about our courtship and the long years of waiting before we could get married and how young we had been. I talked about the farm and the good times we had there.

I talked for hours. Talked about the silly things, the good things, the times that I had cherished, about everything that had been important to me in our life together. I held his hand and poured my heart out. I told him over and over again how much I loved him and how happy he had always made me.

I do not even know if he heard me. The last words he said to me were, "Oh, Joyce. Sit down."

Finally they came and told me I had to leave. It was way after midnight. I kissed him once more and left.

I set my alarm for seven to go back to the hospital, but the telephone woke me a little before six. It was Dr. Foley, and I knew it was terrible because she had never called before.

Milt was dead. He had just died. I took it calmly. It did not seem real. Milt could not die. Not after all he had been through. But it was real. He was dead.

Dr. Foley told me the hospital would hold Milt's body until I came. It was so strange to think of him as being a body now, no longer a man. But when I walked into his room, it was still Milt lying there in the bed. He looked peaceful. The cruel lines of pain had left his face.

They left me alone with him. I kissed him. I kissed his hands and I kissed his eyes and I kissed his head and I cried. I told him how much I loved him, and I said good-bye. Then they came to take him away.

Before I left the hospital, I asked permission to use the office, and I called *The New York Times* and gave them information for his obituary. It appeared in the paper the following day. I was very pleased when I read it. I felt that it honored Milt in death as he deserved.

Dr. Milton J. Brothers, Diabetes Specialist, 62

Dr. Milton J. Brothers, an internist who specialized in the treatment of diabetes, died of bladder cancer yesterday at Memorial Sloan–Kettering Cancer Center. He was 62 years old and lived in Fort Lee, N.J.

Dr. Brothers, the husband of Dr. Joyce Brothers, the psychologist, was co-chief of the diabetes clinic at Mt. Sinai Medical Center and associate clinical professor at the center's medical school. He was also chief of the diabetes unit at the Veterans Administration Hospital in the Bronx.

Dr. Brothers, a native of Jamaica, Queens, held bachelor's and master's degrees from Cornell University. He received his medical degree from the Downstate Medical Center of the State University of New York in Brooklyn. He served in the Navy in World War II.

In addition to his wife, he is survived by a daughter, Dr. Lisa Arbisser of Davenport, Iowa; a sister, Marjorie Uman of Lake Worth, Fla., and four grandchildren.

PART 2

~⚜~

THROUGH THE
TUNNEL OF GRIEF

Seven

There was no time for grief, no time for crying. There were only details. There were people to notify—the family, friends, Milt's colleagues, his office nurses, so many people. Flowers to order. Food for the people who would come back to the apartment after the funeral. There was the funeral itself to arrange.

I had always thought funerals a barbaric custom. Now, as a widow, I found the ceremony helpful. You have to hold yourself together. You cannot fall apart. There is too much to be done. Some parts of your routine have to continue. You have to dress. You have to put on makeup. You have to greet everyone. You have no time to cry. Arranging the funeral and going through the ceremony keep you going at a time when you are numbed and in shock.

That numbness is the first stage of grief for most people. For me, it was a blessing. I did everything I was supposed to do. I was busy, busy, busy. But I felt nothing. It was almost as if I had been replaced by a robot that had been programmed to cope. And coping was indeed the order of the day.

Raffi, Lisa's father-in-law, had been staying with me, and he was a pillar of quiet strength. There is nothing more helpful than having someone who cares about you help handle the details. For instance, when I went to see the funeral director to make the arrangements, Raffi looked at caskets and picked out three for me to choose from. I had dreaded the idea of having to look at dozens of caskets and listen to the salesman tell me about their features and prices. This way I only had to look at three and choose the one I liked best.

I was relieved that we had a family burial plot and that I did not have to rush out and buy one, but all of a sudden I was in the middle of misunderstandings and hurt feelings. I had always thought Milt and I would be buried together in my family's plot at Beth David Cemetery on Long Island. Everyone is there, my father, my grandparents, and my uncles and aunts. There was room for my mother, for Milt and me, for my sister, Elaine, and her husband, and for Lisa and her husband.

But Milt's sister, Margie, wanted him to be buried

next to their mother in their family plot. That would have meant that when I was buried I would have to be away from my mother and dad, and I could not face that. So I begged Margie to understand. And, mercifully, she did. But this was a hurdle that I had not expected.

My mother was another unexpected hurdle. She had worked out who was to be buried where in our plot, but the way she had worked it out was that if Milt was buried in the spot she had chosen, eventually one couple in the family would have to be separated.

So I had to draw up a diagram to show Mother, who had not been very well for the last few years, that there was a way every husband and wife could be buried side by side. She spent hours poring over it, and finally, since she understood that it was important for me, she agreed.

Choosing people to deliver the eulogies at the funeral was one of the most difficult tasks, requiring the skills of a diplomat. I had wanted to have everyone who cared for Milt—and felt like it—say a few words, but the funeral director explained that if the eulogies went on for more than a few minutes, there would be a delay at the cemetery, because the gravediggers had a union-mandated lunch hour. I could not ask people to stand around in the January cold waiting for the gravediggers to finish lunch, so I decided to just have the rabbi and two of Milt's friends deliver eulogies.

I had particularly wanted Milt's best friend to speak, but Raffi advised me that in a Jewish ceremony, the proper thing is to choose people who knew Milt as a doctor and as a teacher as well as a friend. So I chose Dr. Georgio Nicolis, who had known Milt as an academician, a teacher, and a clinician, and Dr. Walter Sencer, who knew him as a friend and a physician.

There were dozens of problems, some trivial, some practical, some involving the rampant emotionalism and injured feelings that are par for the course at the great watersheds of family life—marriage, the birth of your children, and fatal illness and death. I just plowed ahead, blindly coping with them one after the other. I don't remember most of them.

There are lots of things about those days that I don't remember. I don't even remember what I wore to the funeral. I know that Margie and Lisa were in the bedroom and I started pulling things out of the closet and asking them what I should wear. They chose something they considered appropriate. I wore it, and afterward I threw it away.

Nor do I remember my final good-bye to Milt. My mother told me that they gave me time to be alone with him in the funeral parlor. His casket was open. I was there so long that Mother eventually went in to be sure I was all right. She said she found me there patting Milt's head.

. . .

At the service Dr. Nicolis and Dr. Sencer spoke about Milt in all of his aspects. Some of what they had to say was serious and some of it was funny and some of it was very sweet. I was pleased and comforted, but I still wished that all of Milt's friends who cared could have spoken—more for my sake than for theirs. I was hungry to hear people talk about Milt.

The rabbi addressed part of his eulogy to our ten-year-old grandson. He turned to him and said, "Micah, I am going to tell you a secret. Do you remember when you would go to the farm and pan for gold in the streams? Remember how on every visit you always found some?

"Well, it was not because you were such a great prospector. The truth is that your grandfather bought 'fool's gold' and left it there for you to find. The pleasure you experienced in finding it gave him even more pleasure, so great was his love for you. To give you joy gave him joy."

Micah was patently shocked, but as the rabbi went on to say, "Your grandfather loved you deeply. You were special in his eyes, for you were the *zeen* [the son], as so many years ago he himself was the *zeen*," he understood and accepted the loving deception of the "gold" as evidence of his grandfather's love for him.

The worst moment of the funeral came at the cemetery when the coffin was lowered into the ground.

I had not shed a tear up to this time, but now I started sobbing. There is nothing worse than watching the coffin being lowered into the grave. Milt was gone. All that remained—his cancer-ravaged body—was going into this raw, frozen ground.

After that, the ceremony of putting earth on the coffin, which I had dreaded, was not really terrible. One of the attendants hands you a shovel. You do not take it as if you were going to dig up a garden patch or shovel snow. You turn it over and take just a little bit of earth on the tip of the back of the shovel. The small amount is to show how reluctant you are to do it, to finally consign this beloved person to the earth. I have no words to describe my feelings as I dropped the few grains of earth onto Milt's coffin. It was such a solemn moment, such a final act.

Minutes later we all left the cemetery, drifting out slowly. The light was cold that winter noon. It was like being on another planet where nothing existed but cold and death. I looked back once. The grave-diggers had started filling up the hole.

There was barely time to get home and have a cup of blessedly hot tea before people started to arrive. Suddenly the apartment was full of family and friends, some I had not seen for years. Everyone was smiling and talking and sharing anecdotes about Milt. It would have been a lovely party—except that Milt was not there.

Finally everyone left except Margie and Lisa, who

had rushed to New York the day Milt died with her three-day-old baby. They had offered to stay a few days until I got my feet under me again. We were exhausted, three grieving women. We had lost a brother, a father, a husband. It was over. There was nothing more to do. I was still so numb and stunned that I had no idea what had hit me. I went to bed and fell asleep immediately.

The day after the funeral, we moped around the apartment. We had thought we might make a start on sorting out Milt's things, but none of us was able to face it. We could not settle down to anything. We just sat around.

I felt as if I were in a no-man's-land between two lives—the familiar that was now forever lost to me and the unknown that I dreaded. In a way I regretted I was not sitting shiva. It would have provided a transition between the old and the new. But Milt had made me promise not to. Although he believed in God, he was not particularly religiously observant. He felt that this age-old custom was cruel and depressing. "I want you to get out and keep busy," he had told me. "That's what you'll need. Sitting shiva won't do me any good, and it will just be an additional strain on you." I am not sure he was right, but it was important to me to do as Milt had wanted.

Late that afternoon I got a call from *The Pat Sajak Show*. They had no idea that Milt had died, and they wanted to know if I could come to Los Angeles and do a restaurant critique on the show that Friday. I said I would call them back, and then I consulted Lisa and Margie.

"What do you think?" I asked. "Should I do this?" I was tempted. The chance to get out of the apartment was like being given a chance to break out of jail.

"Do it. Please," Lisa said. She was emphatic. "There is nothing you can do here now except fall apart. I have to go home anyway. Amir is alone with Micah and the girls."

"It is the best thing in the world you could do right now," Margie added. "Milt wouldn't want you to be dragging around here doing nothing."

They were right, I told myself. Milt would have said the same thing. So I called back and said I would do the show. I left early the next morning for Los Angeles. When I got to the studio, I practically went into shock. The script called for me to be out on a date with the announcer at the restaurant that I was going to critique. A date! I was horrified, but there was no way I could back out. The segment was scheduled to be shot live in twenty minutes. It would have been too unprofessional.

I hastily explained that my husband had just died and while I understood it was too late to cancel this segment, I just could not seem to be having a date. It would be just too awful. My mind was going a mile a minute trying to come up with an acceptable solution. Finally I hit on the idea of turning it into a spoof.

The producer liked the idea, so we played it funny, as a sort of joke. We did goofy impromptu things like fighting a mock duel at the table with breadsticks and arm wrestling. When the waiter asked me if I had liked the Caesar salad, I said, "It tastes like something left over from the time of Caesar." I am afraid it was not one of television's great moments, although the *Los Angeles Times* found it to be the funniest thing on the show. When I think of it now, I don't know how I got through it. It was so unexpected. Such a booby trap.

Then the Sajak public relations people told the *National Enquirer* about it, and the *Enquirer* ran a story about how Pat Sajak had not known that my husband had just died and how terribly brave I had been and how I had kept the pain and hurt inside in the best tradition of "the show must go on." Well, I hope I managed to conceal the pain, but all the time I was on camera I felt as if I were being mugged.

It was just one of those unfortunate situations, and there was nothing I could have done about it. But in a way, it was good for me. I needed a respite, needed to be out of the apartment. I honestly believe that this "time out," these few hours of distraction, gave me strength to cope with what was to come, for the numbness wore off the minute I got home and walked through the door.

Somehow, in some crazy way, I expected to find Milt there. I dropped my bag in the hall and ran to our bedroom. I knew he would not be there, but I so longed for him to be that I really thought I would find him sitting up in bed reading or watching television.

It was not until I woke up the next morning in the gray January predawn that I really grasped that Milt was dead and gone. He would never hold me again. Never walk through the door again. We would never be together again. We would never laugh together again. Never make plans together again. Plans? I would never make plans again. What was there to plan for? There was no future without Milt.

I got up and made coffee and contemplated the rest of my life with tears streaming down my face.

Eight

Most people think of me as a competent, self-possessed woman, someone who can fly all over the country alone, who can stand in front of a television camera without batting an eyelash, who can deliver a lecture on practically any psychological problem at a moment's notice. And I am all of these things.

But what I really am—or was—is a wife. I devoted three years of courtship and engagement and thirty-nine years of marriage to making Milt happy—and I loved every minute of it. I still fly all over the country. I still appear on television. I still lecture. But on January 9, 1989, I lost my real occupation in life, lost the role I found most fulfilling.

I never lived alone until Milt died. I went from my

father's house to my husband's house. Now I, who had never lived alone, faced a life alone. The man who had been the center of my life for forty-two years was dead. The months ahead were to be the most difficult of my life as I struggled to cope with my grief and forge a new life for myself.

As a psychologist I was familiar with the landmark work of British psychiatrist Dr. Colin Parkes on grief and mourning. "Grief," he wrote, is the only "functional psychiatric disorder whose cause is known, whose features are distinctive and whose course is usually predictable." I had often lectured and written about the course of grief, explaining that each bereaved person goes through a series of stages or reactions and finally arrives at acceptance of his or her loss and at that point is ready to get on with life.

The stages of grief may be predictable, but there is very little that is orderly about a widow's emotions in the weeks and months—sometimes years—following her husband's death. She is caught up in a passionate and painful maelstrom.

The first reaction after her husband's death is almost always shock and then a merciful numbness. This is what carried me through Milt's funeral. When the numbness wears off, however, the pain begins.

This second stage, suffering, is a compound of emotions—longing, panic, helplessness, loneliness, anger, resentment, depression, self-pity, denial. It can be a time of intense psychic misery. But not for all women. Nor do all women experience all these reactions during the second stage. Nor do they experience them with the same intensity.

The second stage may last four months, six months, a year, two years, four years. It varies from woman to woman. And all of this is normal. There are no rules for grief. There is no timetable for grief. There is nothing unloving about the woman who copes with her grief in a matter of months; there is nothing weak or hysterical about the woman who takes several years to reach the third state, that of acceptance.

I emphasize this because the world often makes widows feel guilty. A widow's grief often makes others feel uncomfortable after the first few weeks. They wish she would hurry up and get over it and get back to normal. Or they lift an eyebrow when the widow seems to recover from her grief in an unbecomingly short time. "She must not have loved him all that much," they tell each other.

Such reactions are grossly unfair. Life is hard enough for the widow without her being made to feel guilty for being either too emotional or not emotional enough. There is a biblical phrase that I suggest friends and relatives keep in mind when criticizing the widow: "Judge not, that ye be not judged."

One group of widows seems to arrive at acceptance sooner than others. These are the women who have suffered what psychiatrist Elisabeth Kübler-Ross, author of the classic *On Death and Dying,* calls "windstorms." Dr. Kübler-Ross has found that women "who have gone through a lot of difficulties in life reach a certain degree of acceptance and serenity. They know that death is a part of life, and they take it with incredible serenity and peace." People who have been buffeted by the storms of life seem to emerge from these storms tempered like steel and polished like a diamond. I was not one of those diamonds. I had led a golden life. My years had been full of love and happiness and achievement. Even though I knew all the reactions I would probably experience as I mourned for Milt, I was not prepared for their intensity. I was completely overwhelmed by my grief.

For me, the second stage of mourning was characterized by enormous self-pity, although I did not recognize it as self-pity at the time. The numbness that had encased me ever since Dr. Foley's telephone call to tell me that Milt had died was washed away in a torrent of tears when I got back from doing *The Pat Sajak Show* in Los Angeles.

Crying became almost like breathing or blinking, an automatic, unthinking reaction. Someone would ask me how I was . . . I would pass a restaurant Milt and I used to like . . . I would go to the garage to get my car and see Milt's red Porsche in the next stall . . . I would pick up a document with Milt's signature on it . . . and the tears would start. I cried when I woke up in the morning and he was not there. I cried when—forgetting—I reached out in the middle of the night and he was not there.

It embarrassed me occasionally, because tears make others uncomfortable. As do widows. A weeping widow is as popular as a case of the flu. The standard reaction to a widow's tears is to tell her to stop. "There, there. You mustn't cry. You'll make yourself ill. Tears won't help."

This standard reaction happens to be the worst possible reaction. Tears do help. The widow needs to cry. She will stop when she no longer needs to cry. The fact is that tears are a widow's best friend. They are an early healing device, a kind of emotional first aid.

Tears of sadness or anger contain leucine-enkephalin, one of the brain's natural pain relievers. They also contain prolactin, a hormone that encourages the secretion of tears. (Women have half again as much prolactin as men, which explains in part why women cry more than men do.)

"Before our experiments, which revealed the presence of prolactin and leucine-enkephalin in tears, we had located them in the central nervous system," reported Dr. William Frey II, biochemist and research director of the Dry Eye and Tear Research Center at the St. Paul-Ramsey Center in Minneapolis. "We asked ourselves—what are these brain chemicals doing in tears?"

The answer, Dr. Frey believes, is that crying triggers the brain to release these chemicals. "Crying is an exocrine process," he says, "a process in which a substance—like sweat or urine or feces—comes out of the body, cleansing it of toxic substances. There is every reason to believe crying does the same. Crying does not just feel good, it appears to be an evolutionary device for adapting to emotional stress. When a woman is sad or angry, crying removes the chemicals that build up during stress and helps her feel better."

The value of tears has been recognized from time immemorial, even though no one understood their physiological function until recently. Someone once told me a lovely story from the Talmud that illustrated the importance of tears.

According to the Talmud, when God banished Adam and Eve from the Garden of Eden, Adam protested that the punishment was too severe. They would not be able to cope with the world outside the Garden of Eden.

God considered Adam's plea and found it valid, so he gave Adam and Eve two gifts to help them cope with the hardships of the world. The first gift was the Sabbath for rest and contemplation; the second was the tear.

The widow's tears are varied. There are tears of sadness, of frustration and helplessness, of self-pity, even of anger. All are part of the grief process. And with me they often sprang from self-pity. I was sorry for myself because I had no one to turn to, no one to share things with. There were tears of frustration and helplessness as well. They were usually triggered by trying to deal with the day-to-day, nitty-gritty details of life that I had never had to cope with before. There were all the rotten details pertaining to the funeral and after—where is this document and where is that piece of paper; where do you get death certificates and where do you send them? Every mail delivery seemed to bring more insurance forms, the most labyrinthine documents in the world, to be filled out, a task that could take hours.

I had no idea until I was alone how many things Milt did, details of our life that he took care of automatically. Things he never talked about and I never thought about. I just assumed they were taken care of. I always considered myself extremely competent in managing both my home and my career, but I was only competent in coping with my half.

He used to take care of our cars, checking what he called "the vital body juices." He would see to the water and the oil and the antifreeze and getting them serviced at the garage. I had never had to do anything except put the key in the ignition and occasionally pull into a filling station and tell them to fill it up. After he died I did not know where to put the oil in my car or how much air to put in the tires, when or where to get it serviced.

One weekend at the farm, my sister asked me how to turn on the water heater. I burst into tears. "The secret of doing that died with Milt," I sobbed. I felt so helpless. It turned out to be a simple matter of flicking a switch, but Milt had always taken care of this and a dozen other chores.

It was months before I felt halfway competent to deal with all these things, and even now there are frequent tears of frustration and helplessness when one of the bathroom tiles falls out or the toilet keeps running or the kitchen faucet drips or the fireplace starts belching smoke out into the room and I don't know how to fix it and I am full of self-pity because if I want it fixed, I will have to do it myself. But I have learned what to do. I dry my tears and go out and buy yet another how-to book.

Even when I managed to cope with something and had a certain feeling of triumph, there was often a twist that wiped out the triumph. The summer after Milt died, I mastered the riding mower and mowed the grass around the house in the country. When I finished I drove the mower into the barn, and the front wheels sank through a rotten plank. I had to get someone to lift the front end of the tractor out of the hole. There is no how-to book that tells you how to deal with this kind of disaster.

And there was no how-to book to tell me how to dry up my tears. Disposing of Milt's clothes produced a Niagara. There were so many memories involved. I could not face this task for months.

Once when I was away from home, I had bought Milt a Burberry raincoat. This is a rather expensive item, and Milt was really pleased, especially because there was no reason for my giving it to him. It was not his birthday, not an anniversary; it was just a present, a surprise.

One day at the hospital, his doctor saw Milt's Burberry and said, "You certainly do yourself well. I don't have a Burberry." Milt told him that I had bought it for him, and the doctor said, "Nobody ever loved me enough to buy me a Burberry." Every time I remembered this I would cry.

Then there were all the robes and pajamas I had bought for Milt when he was sick. Every time I went out of town, I used to buy him a robe or slippers or something, just so he would know I had been thinking of him. Now, there were all these wonderful, practically unused clothes. I thought of keeping them. I would sleep in his pajama tops and have the robes shortened. But it was a silly idea. Milt was so tall and broad-shouldered, I would swim in his pajama tops and robes.

It was almost ten months after he died before I could bring myself to give them and the rest of his clothes to Goodwill. And this, of course, triggered bitter tears—tears when I emptied his closet and drawers, tears when I folded everything and stuffed it into the green plastic bags, tears when the Goodwill man came to take the bags away. It was shattering, heart-wrenching, to see his life packed up in a bunch of plastic garbage bags.

One of the hardest things was going through his

wallet. I had put it off and put it off, but one day I needed the registration for his car, and I finally had to go through the wallet. There was some money, the usual cards, the registration, and—this unleashed another torrent of tears—a miniaturization of the electrocardiogram that had been made when he developed the heart flutter. He had always carried it with him in case he had a heart problem away from home.

I kept the wallet and I kept the key he carried in it. It was on a key chain that has a little gadget so that if you clap your hands, it plays music and you know where it is. And that brought back a happy memory that, of course, made me cry.

It was a memory of one summer day at the farm. We were sitting around the kitchen table having lunch. Lisa and her husband and their children were there. Talya must have been almost three at the time, and she said, "Grandpa, you have music coming from your pocket."

We all thought this was so sweet and imaginative of her. Then she said it again—"There's music in your pocket"—and Milt suddenly realized that her voice was of a pitch that triggered the key chain gadget and that there really was music in his pocket.

The farm, which is the place where we had been happiest, is still the most difficult for me, even after all this time. I have managed to adjust to the apartment, but there is not a single dish, chair, rake, mop, or light fixture at the farm that we did not buy together, not a single room or closet that we did not work on together.

I open the refrigerator and remember when we did not have one and kept food in a Styrofoam cooler. The coffee, flour, and sugar containers were an anniversary present from Milt. We found the headboard of our bed in an antique shop and cleaned it up and polished it ourselves. There is not a single thing at the farm that does not have some memory of Milt. And I cry because all I have now are memories.

I wallowed in memories day after day, week after week, month after month. There was no getting away from the memories. I went over everything we had done, everything he had said, the way he walked, the brusqueness he occasionally assumed to hide his sensitivity. All that was left of my marriage was this memory bank. And I kept running these memories through my head. I could not stop. I went through months of obsessive remembering. And every memory triggered tears.

I do not want to give the impression that my tears and self-pity were nonstop, or that I sat around the house crying night and day. Not at all. I soon was back on my usual hectic schedule of writing, lecturing, broadcasting, and so on. And when I was working, I could forget how miserable I was. I would find myself laughing at something and think, Oh! I'm laughing! How nice that I'm not crying.

But the busy, busy life of work only postponed my grief. It did not dissolve it. It was waiting there on the doorstep to greet me every night.

I had thought that the pain would lessen in time. Every morning I woke up and hoped it would be less, but it was not. That was the strange thing—it was not getting any less. Sometimes it was more painful than it had been the previous week. Sometimes I thought I was in worse shape than I had been in the first weeks after Milt died, and this worried me a lot.

There are studies showing that the people who best survived the Holocaust were those who did not remember anything about it. They seemed to have total amnesia on this one subject. They did not even have any recollection of dreaming about it. The men and women who adjusted best had simply walled off the whole experience.

I worried because everything in my life still referred back to Milt. It was like having a nonstop conversation with him in my head. I was afraid that I would never be able to adjust to his death, afraid that there was something wrong with me.

My fears were an indication of just how irrational a quite rational widow can be. I say irrational because the Holocaust and my marriage were opposite ends of a spectrum of emotion and experience. The Holocaust was a hell on earth; my marriage was a kind of heaven. There was no way one's reaction to these could be equated. There was every reason to block memories of the first and every reason to remember the second.

I also knew, intellectually if not emotionally, that this kind of remembering, this repetition, was the only way of coming to terms with what you had lost and realizing that you had lost it forever and now you must go on. Sigmund Freud recognized this when he wrote, rather paradoxically, that remembering was the best way to forget. It is as if each time you remember, a healing film grows over the memory until eventually it is no longer a raw wound. You are whole and healthy again. There may be a scar, but you are ready to forge ahead in life.

The memories and the tears they provoke are partners in the healing process. Tears are not only physically helpful, making the widow feel better; they are psychologically helpful as well. The more a widow cries and eases the pain of her loss with tears, the more she becomes conditioned to her loss. Becoming conditioned to it reduces its pain. There comes a time when she can think of her husband without pain, without tears.

It was nearly a year before I was able to think of Milt without crying, and even then I could not be sure. The turning point came when I remembered how Milt used to call me the Cabinet Lady. And I smiled despite the pain.

The pain had been very real and physical. I had hit my head on an open kitchen cabinet door, so hard that it raised a bump. I tend to leave the cabinet doors open when I am cooking, as I reach in for this and that. Milt used to come into the kitchen and say, "I see the Cabinet Lady is here; you're going to hurt yourself one of these days," as he closed the doors. And I always said, "But I'm too short to hit my head on them." And I never did.

Then this day I ran head-on into an open cabinet door and raised a huge bump on my forehead. After the "Ouch!" I smiled as I thought how he would have enjoyed pointing out that he had warned me a million times about leaving those doors open.

Other memories still provoke tears. One morning, for instance, when I was at the farm, I went down-stairs to make breakfast. I looked at the coffeepot and thought of how much pride Milt used to take in making coffee every morning. I touched the coffee-pot, almost as if I were caressing it, and thought, Poor Rabbit. I miss you so much. And the tears came trickling down.

But these were different tears. This time I was crying for *his* loss, not my own. Up to this time my tears had mostly been for myself. I was the one who was left without love, without companionship, without Milt. I was the one who had to cope with the detritus of my life. I was the one who somehow had to pull myself together and stumble on. I was desperately sorry for myself.

But now I was crying for all Milt had lost. He should have had another twenty years or more of the life he relished so much. It was a turning point. The months of self-pity were coming to an end, but the loneliness went on and on.

Nine

ꙮ

"Oh lonesome's a bad place," wrote poet Kenneth Patchen. And it is. A terrible place. An angry place. It is a kind of hell.

When someone who understood the stages of grief asked me if I felt angry at Milt, I was shocked. Angry with my beloved husband? Never! But I was.

Whenever I thought about his having smoked all those years when he knew very well that cigarettes can kill, I was enraged. He had lost a wonderful life full of people he loved and who loved him all because of those lousy cigarettes. But this was a transitory anger. I knew that he had tried to stop smoking time and time and time again. I knew he did not want to die. I knew he loved me. Loved our life. Loved his work. And even though I cried angry tears whenever

I thought of how we could still be enjoying life together if only he had stopped smoking twenty years
ago, I have never been able to stay mad at Milt. I
used to boil up at things he did or said, but ten minutes later we would be laughing together. There was
no way, I told myself, that I would stay angry with
Milt now. You can't kiss and make up and laugh
with a dead man.

Nevertheless I was full of anger. I was startled by
its intensity. I was angry—not at Milt, but at his
death. I was angry because I missed him bitterly,
because I knew there would never be anyone else
that important in my life, because I hated being a
widow, because I was frightened, because I felt alone
in the world. And much of the time I was angry at
that world.

One morning when I saw a couple with two children piling into a station wagon outside my apartment house, ready to go off for the weekend, I was
consumed by fury, because they were so privileged
and I was not. I became very conscious of couples—
in restaurants, on planes, at the supermarket, reg-
istering at hotels, walking down the street, going to
the movies. Holding hands. Talking intimately.
Smiling at each other. Eating together. Going home
together. Everyone seemed to be part of a couple—
except me. I was all alone, and I hated it. Whenever
I saw a couple who seemed irritated at each other, I
would think, Oh, God, how can you be so annoyed

with each other? If you only knew what it will be like when he is gone.

I used to get angry when I read the obituaries in the morning paper. The men all seemed to be in their seventies and eighties. Milt was only sixty-two. Why couldn't *he* have had those extra ten or twenty years?

I was angry because so much of my life died with him. I kept thinking that just when we had gotten our life all buttoned down, it fell apart. We had a wonderful daughter and wonderful grandchildren. We had no financial problems. We had the farm that we both loved. There were so many things we looked forward to doing together. Our life was truly golden. Now all this had been snatched away from me.

Many widows, perhaps most widows, go through a period of stormy rage at their husbands. "I was furious at him for dying," one woman said. "Leaving me with two small children and a puppy and a mortgage. What was I going to do? How could he do this to me?"

An older woman told me she was overwhelmed by guilt because she was angry with her late husband so much of the time. "I blame him for every little thing that goes wrong in my life. When I drop a glass and it breaks . . . when the furnace goes off . . . when the man does not come to fix the leak in the roof . . . when the car needs a new muffler . . . when my library book is overdue . . . when I gain five pounds, I get furious at him.

"Sometimes I yell out loud, 'You goddamned son of a bitch! You left me all alone to deal with this shit!' And he is dead and gone, the man I loved, still love. I would never, never have yelled at him this way when he was alive. I am shocked when these words come out of my mouth. I feel ashamed of myself. And guilty. So very guilty."

Other widows turn their anger onto the outside world, lashing out at anyone and everyone. They find fault with the doctor who treated their husband. They become outraged because a friend is not able to attend the funeral. They take offense at the most inoffensive remarks. They quarrel with their families. They snap at the neighbors.

All this is completely out of character. In many cases the widow is fighting an unconscious battle to avoid facing the real target of her anger—her husband, who has died and left her alone. She would feel like a monster if she were to unleash her anger on him. The guilt would be unbearable.

But there is no reason for guilt. Loneliness and anger go together like salt and pepper. Loneliness stresses the system, and stress causes red blood cells to clump together, says psychiatrist John Larson, director of the Institute of Stress Medicine at Norwalk Hospital in Connecticut. "This clumping," he says, "deprives the muscle, nerve, and other tissues of nutrients. It is this deprivation of certain brain cells that causes the irritability associated with stress.

The brain cells simply do not have the nutrients they need."

Considering the physical consequences of loneliness and the psychological consequences of loss, anger is practically unavoidable, and there is no reason for a widow to feel guilty when her anger is focused on her late husband.

It is only natural to be angry when something you love or need is taken away from you. A wife becomes angry when the most important person in her world leaves her and, overnight, she becomes a widow.

She is angry because her husband has died and his death has deprived her of love and understanding and companionship. She is angry because she is emotionally insecure, because she is financially insecure. She is angry because her very identity has been eroded, because she has lost status. She is angry because she has to cope with all these losses when she is in the black depths of loneliness. She is angry at her husband because he died and left her in this miserable situation.

Make no mistake about it. Widows are among our country's most oppressed minorities. When it comes to social status, "widows are losers on all counts," says sociologist Helena Lopata. "Widowhood means a plunge in social status in our society, which still bases a woman's worth on her relationships with men."

Lopata is not alone in believing that a woman's social status is largely contingent on her having a man in her life, even in these days of enlightened feminism. Eighty-eight percent of women twenty-nine years and older who participated in a study published in *Female Psychology* thought of themselves as social rejects. The majority of them took this dim view of themselves because they were not married. As one of the participants in the study told the researchers, "An unmarried woman can achieve high professional status, but only the married woman attains high social status."

I am very fortunate in that my work constantly reaffirms that I am a person of some status, a worthwhile person. Yet there were times after Milt died when I worried about my professional status.

For instance, I had a tentative commitment to be on an important nighttime talk show. I called and asked if we could firm up the date. "I'll have to check with the producer," the scheduler told me. "I'll call you back this afternoon."

She did not call me back. Ordinarily this would not have bothered me. Producers change their minds. People get canceled. It is no big deal. There is always another show. But then, just six months after Milt's death, it bothered me a lot. I decided they did not want me on the show after all, that nobody would ever want me on a show again. I was terribly depressed and discouraged.

The scheduler called the next morning and gave me a choice of two dates. She apologized for not calling earlier and explained that the producer had been in meetings all the previous afternoon and she had not been able to check with him until that morning.

Why had I been so upset? A year ago I would not have given the incident a second thought. I was simply insecure, not as sure of my status as I had been before.

I had not expected to become a member of a minority group after Milt died, but I did. When a woman is divorced, there is a sense that she has failed. While people do not consider a widow to be a failure, they do view her as less fortunate than they, and for this reason they have less respect for her. The result is often that old friends drop the widow, and families tend to treat her with less consideration.

While Milt and I had been used to seeing a small circle of couples, I found I felt uncomfortable with them after he died. In my own case, perhaps partly due to my celebrity status as well as their friendship for me, I did continue to hear from these couples, but much less frequently. One evening several months after Milt's death, I was driven to searching angrily through the bookcases for a book I had read some twenty years ago, Konrad Lorenz's landmark work, *On Aggression*.

I was looking for a particular passage that I remembered vaguely, a passage that described the way I felt life had been treating me since Milt died. When

I found the book, I riffled through the pages until I found the passage.

"From the moment a goose realizes that the partner is missing," Lorenz had written, "it loses all courage and flees even from the youngest and weakest geese. As its condition quickly becomes known to all the members of the colony, the lonely goose rapidly sinks to the lowest step in the ranking order."

Yes, this was what I had remembered, and it made me furious. In the human ranking order, the widow becomes a second-class citizen unless she fights against it. And fight she should if she does not want to sink to that "lowest step in the ranking order." If she does not, the feeling of inferiority that is forced upon her will only deepen her loneliness.

My anger became a spur to get on with life. That night, sitting on the floor next to the bookcase, I promised myself that I was not going to be a lonely goose, that I would not permit myself to "sink to the lowest step in the ranking order."

It was a brave promise, and I was not always able to keep it, but the thought of that lonely goose who had lost her courage as well as her mate gave me strength not only to resist any diminishing of my status, social or professional, but to eventually stop being so passive. Instead of expecting people to keep on including me in their lives, I began to take steps to include them in my life.

For instance (and I admit it was well over a year before I was able to push myself to do it), I invited two of the couples Milt and I used to see to have lunch at the farm one Sunday.

It was a wonderful day. After lunch we walked along the dirt road that runs past the farm, threw pebbles in the brook, and admired my neighbor's herd of cows. It was an easy and relaxed afternoon. We had a lot of catching up to do. We shared our memories of Milt and the pleasure he took in everything associated with the farm. There were a few tears and a lot of laughter. This get-together broke the ice, and we now see each other—not as often as we used to, but often enough.

Other widows have confirmed my experience of social isolation. They tell me that married couples who had been longtime friends drop away little by little. They are no longer considered a member of the group. People no longer pick up the telephone and say, "Jack and I are going to the movies. Want to join us?" or, "If you're not doing anything, why don't you come over for supper Sunday night?"

"My telephone just stopped ringing a few weeks after Eldon's funeral," one widow told me. "It was as if, in their eyes, I had died, too. I feel ostracized. I understand it. They are afraid I'm going to steal their husbands. But I don't like it. I resent it."

Another widow told me, "My old friends started to treat me like a servant. The winter my husband died, one woman started leaving her two kids with me weekends so she and her husband could go skiing. 'I know you must be lonely,' she would tell me as if *she* were the one who was doing the favor. Another couple started leaving their baby with me Friday nights when they went to the movies. They simply assumed that I would be home with nothing to do. When it dawned on me that they were not going to include me in any of their activities, I got quietly mad and stopped letting myself be cast as an unpaid baby-sitter.

"And these were my friends!" she exclaimed.

An attractive widow in her late forties said, "The weirdest thing happened a couple of months after Kevin died. My best friend's husband dropped in on his way home from work one evening and started coming on to me. He would never have made a pass at me while my husband was alive. What made him think that he could now? Or that I would be interested? I was furious and let him know it. And you know what he said? He said, 'You ought to be grateful.'

"What it adds up to," she said, "is that I have been consigned to a minority group—that of women without men. In some ways I don't mind. I have wonderful women friends, bright and funny and helpful. I have always had good women friends. But why have I been dropped by the married world? It makes me wonder if they ever really were my friends."

A widow does not have to be a second-class citizen, but she will be if she does not take charge of her own life. Passivity is her worst enemy. The early months of widowhood are booby-trapped with status attacks. The widow never knows where or how she will be attacked next. Her only defense is to be aware of the danger, since the "attackers" often act out of love.

Friends and relatives start treating you like a child. They do not hesitate to tell you what to do and how to do it, as if you were no longer capable of managing your life. And perhaps you do not know what you want to do or what you should do. You need time to think, to adjust to your new situation.

The wisest advice one can give a widow is, Do not make any changes in your life or any important decisions for at least a year. A widow, of course, does not always have the luxury of time when it comes to making changes or major decisions like moving. But if she can, a woman will do well to just stay put for a year or so until she gets herself sorted out.

Having warned against making hasty decisions, I must confess that as a psychologist who was well aware of the danger of hasty decisions, I made one just weeks after Milt died that I regretted almost immediately. Fortunately there was a happy ending to the episode.

This is what happened. Milt had a big farm tractor. It was the pride of his life. When Micah was seven or eight, Milt had taught him how to run the tractor, and one of my happiest memories is of my skinny little grandson perched on the monster tractor, proud as can be, with Milt walking alongside to make sure nothing went wrong.

After Milt died I sold the tractor to my neighbors, thinking that I would never use it.

A few months later, I was on the television show, *Live—Regis & Kathie Lee*. Regis asked me if I had any advice for widows, and I said, "Don't make any quick changes in your life. Wait a few months, wait a year. Then you will know better what you want and need to do."

"Did you make any changes you regretted?" he asked.

"I sold my husband's tractor," I said, "and I am sorry I did."

When the show was over, they told me I had a telephone call. It was my neighbor. She said, "You can have the tractor back if you want it." I planned to learn how to run it, and I knew that once I did, the memory of Milt would be riding on it right along with me.

I was confronted with a major decision almost immediately after the funeral. Lisa and Amir urged me to go live with them in Iowa. "We have plenty of room," Lisa assured me. "You can be absolutely independent."

"And you can travel just as easily from here as from New York," Amir pointed out.

They were quite right. Their house was large

enough that we would not get in each other's way. And in some ways there were advantages to living in the middle of the country, since many of my trips would be shorter.

But it would not be my house or my life. Lisa and Amir loved their life in Davenport, but I was a New Yorker born and bred. I was not sure that I could adapt. Not sure that I *wanted* to adapt.

I was very comfortable in the apartment. There was plenty of room for my office and my secretaries, and it was only minutes away from the television and broadcasting studios in Manhattan. I could not duplicate this convenience in my daughter's house. Nor could I see moving a thousand miles away from the farm, which was such an important part of my life.

I thanked them and said that much as I loved them and adored my grandchildren, I thought I would be better off staying where I was. The clincher was that I felt I would lose my independence if I moved in with them—even though I knew they would bend over backward not to interfere in my life.

I had been tempted by their offer. It would have been wonderful to be able to see them and my grandchildren every day, but I had recently done research for one of my columns on the depression syndrome that doctors call "the moving-to-be-near-their-daughters syndrome." And this research contributed in part to my decision.

I had learned that for many widows, and particularly the elderly, loneliness is linked not with how seldom they see their children and grandchildren, but with the absence of their peers, friends, and acquaintances. An older widow who moves halfway across the country to be close to her daughter can be very lonely because nothing is familiar—the shops, the library, the doctor, the dentist. She no longer sees her old friends, and she often finds it difficult to make new friends in the new community.

If she has moved in with her daughter, her situation may be even worse. She has not only left her home and her friends, she has lost part of her identity. She is no longer running the household. She begins to feel like a fifth wheel. Instead of the comfort she expected to find, the move has simply added stress to stress.

According to the life-change ratings developed by psychiatrist Thomas Holmes, which put a stress value on significant life changes, the loss of a spouse is the most stressful event in a person's life. Dr. Holmes gives it a rating of 100 life-change units. Add to that:

change in living conditions	25 units
change in residence	20 units
change in social activities	18 units
revision of personal habits	24 units

These changes, common for a widow who moves some distance from her home to live with or close to her daughter, add up to 187 life-change units. If there has also been a change in her financial status, that adds another 38 units—a grand total of 225 life-change units.

Two hundred life-change units during the course of a year represents more stress than most people can handle. Dr. Holmes recommends that people under this much stress seek help from a trusted physician or therapist.

Women should also be aware that families are sometimes brutally unkind to the older widow, because they—consciously or unconsciously—consider her less powerful and less important than when her husband was alive. They become impatient and thoughtless. They treat her with less respect and consideration. One letter I received from an elderly widow who experienced just this kind of treatment from her family made me cry.

"Since I have been a widow," she wrote, "my children think they can say anything they like to me. They treat me like a child or someone who's not all there. They would never have treated me this way when their father was alive. Now they think they can run my life. It makes me mad, but there's nothing I can do about it. I am dependent on them now."

Not all changes in status are brutal or anger-provoking. Some are inevitable and would probably have come about anyway. I realized the first Thanksgiving after Milt's death that my status in the family had undergone a change. I had invited them all—

eighteen children and adults—for the Thanksgiving weekend. And as the days passed, I became aware for the first time that my family no longer revolved around me. There had been a quite unconscious changing of the guard.

Milt and I had been the center of the family, and everyone else had been a spoke. Without Milt, I was no longer at the core. Now Lisa and Amir were the center, and I was the family matriarch; I had become a spoke. I realized that this was the way it was going to be from now on.

There was no unkindness or anything of that sort. It was a natural evolution. Everyone was very concerned about me and how I felt. For instance, Lisa's father-in-law's sixty-fifth birthday was that weekend, and Lisa and Amir wanted the children to put on a little play as his birthday present. But they very thoughtfully asked ahead of time if it would bother me. They worried that I might have been upset or hurt since Milt was not there.

I told them honestly that I would not be upset in the least and that the loss of one member, no matter how beloved, should not mean that joy has gone out of the family forever.

At the same time I could not help but think angrily that life was terribly unfair. Why should other people have their lives go on while mine, as I saw it then, had stopped? But I kept this feeling to myself, and it did not prevent me from enjoying the play my grandchildren put on for their other grandfather.

Perhaps only a widow can understand how loss of status intensifies loneliness and spawns anger. I wrote earlier that the widow often becomes an unpleasant person, and no wonder. Only a saint can accept with equanimity the loss of the person she loved and the life she found fulfilling. Looking back, I am shocked at the bitterness and rage I often felt. I am not proud of these feelings, but I had them, and I was not able to pick myself up and start life over again until I had gotten them out of my system.

Ten

My anger eventually dissipated, but my loneliness . . . ah, that was something else. I began to believe I had been condemned to loneliness the way a criminal is condemned to jail. And I wondered if I would survive. Half a year after Milt died, my loneliness had increased to the point where I felt it was eating me alive.

Loneliness has nothing to do with being alone. I was with people all day long. I smiled and I functioned as a normal person—yet I felt as if I were wandering in the wilderness. I could be socializing after giving a lecture, greeting people and responding to questions, but inside I was shivering with loneliness. I could be in the hurly-burly of a book-signing session with people literally breathing down my neck and feel alone in the world. I could be on a television talk show and feel so lonely that I had to fight the tears.

My tears were always close to the surface. One of my loneliest times during the first year was when my plane from Los Angeles or Chicago or wherever would come into New York for a landing. As it circled, I would look out the window and see all the little houses below and think that almost everyone in those houses had someone to come home to, someone she could tell about what happened during her day, her triumphs and her worries. And I did not. I would come home to an empty apartment. And as the plane touched down, I would have tears in my eyes. I could not help it.

Coming home to emptiness was terribly hard. I would unlock the door and turn on the lights. The place was silent. No television on. No music playing. No one talking on the telephone. No one to give me a big hug and a welcome-home kiss.

I would check my answering machine for messages. Even that mechanical voice was a welcome sound. I would get myself something to eat. I never bothered to set a place at the table just for myself. I ate standing up at the kitchen sink. No wonder I lost weight.

When people commented that I had lost weight, I told them I had discovered a new diet—the grief diet, which causes immediate loss of appetite. Most of the time I honestly did not care whether I ate or not. There were other times, however, when I ate like a little pig.

Shortly after Milt died, I went on a veal chop binge. I had never bought veal chops, because Milt did not like them. Now there was no reason not to, so I began cooking them three and four times a week. But the night came when I never wanted to see another veal chop. I looked at the chop I had just taken out of the refrigerator and I said, just as if Milt were right there, "You were absolutely right. I don't like veal chops, either."

For months when I came home from a trip, there were nights when I expected to walk into the apartment and find him there. I *knew* he would not be, but there was always that tiny crazy glimmer of hope that he would be. Almost every widow I have spoken with admits to the same kind of expectation. One woman told me that she was under the dryer one afternoon when she got a very strong feeling that her husband was going to walk into the hairdresser's. He had never been there in their whole married life, but that day she was convinced that he was going to walk in the door any minute.

Some widows smell familiar odors—their husband's tobacco smoke or sweat. One reported sitting on the porch on a Sunday afternoon and suddenly becoming aware of the scent of her husband's after-shave lotion. The fragrance was so strong that she looked up, half expecting to find him standing beside her.

Forty to 50 percent of widows experience hallucinations. They are positive that they see their husband. They see him on the sidewalk as they ride by on the bus. They spot him ahead of them in the checkout line at the supermarket or in a car at a gas station. Of course, when they try to catch up with him, he has disappeared.

These hallucinations are absolutely normal. "Nobody likes to talk about them," says Dr. Robert Ostroff, clinical professor of psychiatry at Yale, "because they think they're going crazy when it happens. But it is simply part of a normal grief reaction."

In the first months after Milt's death, I used to dream about him several nights a week. The dreams were so real that it seemed as if he were there with me. In them, he was always angry with me, the way he had been in the last months of his life, but I did not care. I was so happy he was there. When I woke up it was as if I had been abandoned all over again, and I felt lonelier than ever.

The nights were bitterly lonely. Sleep was hard to come by. Some nights I would lie there staring into the dark until the first gray of dawn. Other nights I would fall asleep right off and wake up a couple of hours later and not be able to get back to sleep the rest of the night.

I learned to keep a selection of books on my bedside table for the sleepless nights. I read straight through the *New York Times* fiction best-seller list and then through the nonfiction list. I longed for Milt so much that my mind played tricks on me. I would be reading in bed and come across a fact or an idea that fascinated me and turn automatically to share it with him—and then realize all over again that he was no longer there to share things with. And each time this happened, loneliness would shake my heart the way a chill shakes one's body.

Weekends and anniversaries were and are the worst. No one warns the widow of how ghastly lonely and depressing they are. I used to dread every holiday, every Saturday and Sunday, every anniversary. I had no defense against the loneliness that invaded me on these days. Each one reminded me of how much I had lost and how much my life had changed.

My weekends were so empty that whenever an opportunity arose for me to give a Saturday or Sunday lecture or be on radio or television, I jumped at it. Other weekends were a kind of purgatory, a punishment that had to be endured, until I started working on this book and spending my free weekends at my desk in the city. I hoped that putting my grief down on paper would help me. And it has.

It has forced me to face my feelings and understand

that literally millions of other women have felt the same way and survived. I have been shocked to realize how self-centered and absorbed I became in the early months, so self-centered that I was not aware of how desolate Lisa felt. She had adored her father, and his loss was an emotional earthquake for her. Nor was I aware of how very grief-stricken Milt's office nurse was. She had been with him for years and years. We thought of her as part of the family. Both Lisa and the nurse were very supportive and comforting. I wish now that I could have been more supportive and comforting of them. One loses sight of the fact that it is not only the widow who suffers. Everyone who loses a beloved person suffers.

Writing the book also helped me realize, much to my astonishment, that my grief was subsiding. I could hardly believe how markedly my sadness, my depression, my fears, my anger, my loneliness, have diminished as the months dragged by. They have not disappeared entirely, but I am healing. And I know it. Without this chronicle, I do not think I would be aware of it.

Difficult as weekends were that first year, the anniversaries and holidays were far worse. Milt and I had always been very sentimental. Even after nearly four decades of marriage, we still celebrated every little anniversary, every holiday. We gave each other silly presents. We went out for dinner. We were as foolish as kids. And loved every minute of it.

Valentine's Day, barely a month after Milt's funeral, was heartbreaking. It was then that it really came home to me that there would never be another valentine on my pillow, never be another silly Valentine's Day present. Actually there was a present, but I still have not found the courage to open it.

It came after he died. It might not seem silly to anyone else, but to me it is endearingly silly. One of the things that Milt used to tease me about was that no one had ever invited me to a Tupperware party. His mother had been invited to Tupperware parties. His sister had been invited to Tupperware parties. My sister had been invited to Tupperware parties. But no one had ever asked me to a Tupperware party. So whenever the subject of popularity came up, Milt would say, "What do *you* know about popularity? You've never even been invited to a Tupperware party."

His last silly gift was Tupperware. I know what is in the package, because I had found the Tupperware catalog and a record of the order in the drawer of his bedside table after his death. It is a set of plastic containers that telescope, the way an accordion does. As you use the flour or rice or whatever you are storing, you squish the top of the container down.

One Valentine's Day he gave me a little wind-up mouse that carries a piece of cheese and flips over in a very jaunty way. We always had problems with mice at the farm. Milt used to tell me that since we could not seem to get rid of them, we should pretend they were pets. And they *were* cute. So he gave me that mouse. I found it in my desk the other day and wound it up and watched it race around. It was the first time I have been able to do that since he died.

But that first Valentine's Day was just pure black misery. Somehow it was worse because I knew that Milt had been thinking about me, and the box from Tupperware that I had stashed on the shelf in the hall closet was the very last of the little silly presents.

Milt and I even played Easter bunny to each other. This was a deep, deep secret between the two of us. How can you tell anyone that the Easter bunny brings you presents?

That first Easter after his death, I went out and bought myself a present from the Easter bunny. It was a little ceramic jar with the Big Bad Wolf on the lid. The wolf is wearing granny glasses that are removable. It is perfectly sweet and ridiculous. I keep tea in it. But it did not really help. It was not really a present. It just accentuated the fact that Milt was not there to give me one; it made me feel even lonelier.

The Fourth of July was even worse. It would have been our thirty-ninth wedding anniversary. I spent it alone in bed with a raging fever and a case of the flu. I felt terrible and kept wishing I were dead. If I were dead, I thought feverishly, I would be with Milt. Or if that was not the way things worked in the hereafter, at least I would not be a widow, ill and alone in bed on my wedding anniversary. It did not seem fair that I should be so miserable. I truly was about ready to curl up my toes and die, but my body was not. In a couple of days my temperature was down and I was on the mend. I was a little wobbly and I looked terrible and I just could not see how I was going to live without Milt, but it was obvious that I was going to have to.

A week or two later I remembered the light fixture. The Sunday after our thirty-seventh anniversary, we took two old oxen yokes we had found in the barn to a small shop that had just opened near the farm. We asked the women who ran it if they could make them into a hanging light fixture. They were enthusiastic about the idea and worked out a design we both liked. We spent a lot of time with them choosing bulbs and discussing the best way to electrify it.

As we drove away, we both commented on how pleasant they were and what fun it had been working out all the details of our ox-yoke chandelier.

That Sunday afternoon was the last time we really had fun together. When we got back to the city, Milt went into the hospital for exploratory surgery to find out what was causing the traces of blood in his urine, and they discovered the malignant polyp. From that time on our lives were poisoned by cancer.

Sometime that August I got a note that the chandelier was ready, but I could not leave Milt alone just to drive out to the country to pick it up. Every couple of months they would send another note saying that the chandelier was there waiting for us. But I just could not get myself there. I could not face that happy memory.

Finally—two years later—after I recovered from the flu, I went to pick it up. I walked in and I stood in the middle of the shop and I burst into tears. All I could think of was that Sunday afternoon when we had been so happy. I was terribly embarrassed by my tears. I was afraid the other customers would think I was crying hysterically because I was not happy with the chandelier. So I tried to explain to everyone that I was very pleased with the chandelier and that was not the reason I was crying. Heaven only knows what they thought.

The chandelier is at the farm now, but I still have not gotten around to finding someone to hang it for me. One keeps postponing the painful things.

By the time Thanksgiving came around, I was a little smarter. I had learned how much lonelier one feels on those special days that remind you of all that has gone from your life. This time I planned ahead to make it as easy for myself as I could.

I invited the whole family for the four-day Thanksgiving weekend. There were nineteen of us altogether. That was the weekend I discovered air mattresses. There are five bedrooms at the farm, but not enough beds to go around. So I got air mattresses for the children. They loved the whole business of inflating them at night and then stamping the air out of them in the morning so they could be rolled up and put out of the way.

It was crowded and noisy, but everyone had a good time, even though none of us could forget that this was the first Thanksgiving without Milt. Nor did we want to forget. We talked about him a lot. Lisa told how one Thanksgiving, when for some reason there were only the three of us, he had insisted on having every traditional Thanksgiving dish from creamed onions to turnips, from chestnut stuffing and cranberry sauce to three kinds of pie—and the biggest bird that would fit in our oven. We had leftovers until we just could not face them any longer. The children loved that story. And Amir told how awed he always was by the surgical skill with which Milt carved the turkey. The memories were bittersweet, but there were no tears. Not really. Just a few cases of brimming eyes that were hastily wiped.

I had my own special memories, which I kept to myself. It was too grim a memory to share. A year ago Milt and I had not even thought of celebrating Thanksgiving. He was out of his mind, crazed by the painkilling drugs he had been given. It had been a terrible time. I remember being thankful when we found Dr. Kathleen Foley, who balanced his medications so that he never again became delusional and raving.

That Sunday after they all left, I was flooded with a sense of great relief. It had been so hectic, so busy, so much had been going on, so many people talking all at once, so many children underfoot, so much turmoil and excitement, that, for the first time since Milt died, I was glad to be alone.

Planning ahead and surrounding myself with people had been the right prescription for the anniversary blues. I had been so busy with the cooking and the coping and the guests that my grief had to be put on the back burner.

The really bad anniversary was January 9, the first anniversary of Milt's death. Surrounding myself with family would not help. I told myself I was not going to spend the time wallowing in grief. I just had to get through the day and that was all there was to it. I filled the hours with as many obligations as I could so I would be too busy even to think. I made an appointment with the doctor for a physical checkup. After that I rushed downtown to the Wall Street area for a business conference. Then back to NBC to do my radio show. I stopped in at my publisher's to discuss my progress on this book. In the evening I went back to NBC to do another radio show.

But when I got home that night, I finally had to face my heartbreak. There was no more running away from it.

One year and one day ago, I had sat beside Milt's bed for hours, holding his hand and talking to him about our life and how much he had always meant to me. I never saw him alive again. He died before the next dawn.

The tears I had repressed all day could be denied no longer. I threw myself on the bed and wept. Finally I got up and got ready for bed. I took a bath, put drops in my tear-reddened eyes, and got into bed and cried some more. It was too much. I really thought my heart would break.

Eleven

"**S**he died of a broken heart."

I can remember my grandmother saying this about one of her neighbors who had died a few weeks after her husband's death. I was only eight or nine years old, and at the time I thought the story was terribly romantic. After Milt died I began to wonder if it might really be true. My heart was broken, and there were times when I thought I would die of loneliness.

There are two kinds of loneliness—intimate and social. Intimate loneliness results from the loss of a significant and beloved person. Social loneliness results from being cut off from a group with which one used to have close ties. Most widows suffer from both kinds. The result is what Dr. William A. Sadler, an authority on loneliness in American life, calls "unmitigated complex loneliness." And this can kill.

People do die of broken hearts. Dr. George Engel spent six years of research, examining 170 cases of sudden death, to establish that this is not merely a romantic piece of folklore. He discovered that most sudden deaths fall into one of seven categories, four of them related to the loss of a spouse or child or lover or some other dearly beloved person. These categories are:

1. Sudden death almost immediately after the death of a beloved person.

2. Death within a few hours of the death of a beloved person.

3. Death on or near the anniversary of the death of a beloved person.

4. Sudden death during loss of status or self-esteem, losses that most widows suffer after the death of their husbands.

(The other categories, which are not related to loss and loneliness, are sudden death in a setting of personal danger, sudden death when the danger was over, and sudden death at a moment of great joy or triumph.)

Most of the deaths Dr. Engel investigated were caused by heart attacks, and although some, but by no means all, of the victims had had previous heart problems, Dr. Engel concluded that there was overwhelming evidence that some people do indeed die of broken hearts. Interestingly, the coronary death rate among widows aged twenty-five to thirty-four is *five times* that of married women in the same age group.

Although I felt like walking death for most of the first year after Milt died, I survived. I had no heart attacks, no serious illnesses, but my usual sturdy good health deserted me. After the funeral I came down with a head cold that turned into a chest cold that left me with a cough that lasted for months. When I got over that, I came down with the flu. When I recovered from that, I suffered from a series of minor colds, one after the other.

I had a physical checkup, and the doctor said there was nothing wrong with me. I simply had a galloping case of loneliness. And there is nothing doctors can do about that.

My loneliness sent me to reviewing the literature on the psychology of loneliness. I was struck by some of the conclusions of Dr. Robert Weiss, a sociologist who has been called the father of loneliness research.

"Loneliness that involves yearning for an emotional partner," he wrote, "is based on a conviction that the world is barren of anyone with whom a bond of love and caring can be established. It is a symptom of a specific deficiency in human relationships just as scurvy is a symptom of a specific nutritional deficiency."

He could have been writing about me. I did feel

that there would never be anyone in my life whom I could love and respect as much as I had loved and respected Milt. And there was no doubt but that I suffered from a "deficiency in human relationships."

I had no husband. And I had no close friends. For the first time in my life, I missed having close friends. I know literally hundreds of people, and while I am fond of many of them, I have no real friends. This sounds strange, but true friendship requires a commitment, an investment of time and caring, and all my life I have worked so hard that I never had the time to invest in friendship.

I was like my mother in this respect. Mother was a lawyer, and from the time she married my father until his death, she worked right along with him in his law office. She was a brilliant and beautiful woman. People admired her, but she had no close friends. Her husband, her daughters, her home, and her work filled her life. She had no time for anything more.

When Milt and I married, I fell into the same pattern. Milt was my best friend. I needed nothing more. But now I wish I had made time for friendships. I long for one or two good friends with whom I can talk about Milt and how much I miss him, with whom I can share part of my life, talk about my problems, friends who would rejoice with me at my triumphs. And I in turn would be a part of their lives and share their ups and downs. But I do not have any. And this has contributed to my loneliness.

I do have my family, and I do not know what I would have done without their support, especially Lisa's. But I have become convinced that the research findings that it is more stressful to lose a spouse than a child are absolutely correct.

If you lose your child, your husband shares your grief. The two of you comfort each other. You are not alone.

If you lose your husband, your children may mourn as passionately as you do, but there is a different dimension to their grief. They lost a father; you lost a husband.

If your children are young, you must support and comfort them. They cannot share your grief or comfort you. If your children are grown, they can share your grief to a great extent and they can comfort you, but—as I discovered with my own daughter—the sharing and comforting are limited. They have their own lives and obligations.

Lisa was there for me when I needed her most. She was the only one I could really share my grief with, and that was immensely comforting. But she had a husband and four children, a home to run, a medical practice, patients to see—and she lived a thousand miles away. I could not look to her to mitigate my loneliness.

Nor would it have been fair. Not only did she have a brand-new baby, she had her own grief. She was mourning the loss of the father she adored. She had more than enough stress in her life.

. . .

A widow group had very kindly invited me to join them after Milt's death. They told me how helpful they found it to share their sorrow and their experience and that they had found comfort in the fellowship of other widows.

At that point in my grief, joining a widow group seemed equivalent to accepting the role of the lonely goose. I could not see sharing my grief and my memories of Milt with strangers. I believed that if I were to rehash my feelings with a group of widows, I would be stuck in the same old groove of despair like a needle on an old phonograph record.

I had another reason to hesitate. Celebrity has its rewards, and it has its perils. One of the perils of being Dr. Joyce Brothers, I have learned through experience, is that it is not wise to discuss personal matters with strangers, no matter how sympathetic or understanding they may seem.

I would not have been able to be as frank about my grief and its various manifestations with a group of women I did not know as I can be in this book, where my exact words and the context of each emotion or situation are in black and white. There can be no doubt about what I say, no misinterpretations.

But in an open sharing of emotions and experiences with people I did not know, there would always be the possibility that I would pick up one of the supermarket tabloids and find my name in headlines: DR. JOYCE BROTHERS DREAMS HUSBAND'S GHOST

IS ANGRY. That kind of thing. It would have been professionally and emotionally risky.

Nevertheless there are times when I think I should have accepted, if not that invitation, then some other. There were too many nights when I went to bed early and watched television. It provided an escape from loneliness, but it was only a temporary escape—a few hours of distraction, nothing more.

I probably would have been much better off if I had done something with my evenings—signed up for a course in computers or French or eighteenth-century English literature, joined an exercise class, found a piano teacher (I used to be a competent player), done something, anything, with people who shared my interests. But it all seemed like too much effort. It was easier to get into bed and watch television. I used to tell myself that it was important to watch, to keep up with who was on what show and all that. The truth was, though, that I had always kept up with the new television programs and personalities without staring at the tube for hours on end night after night.

Today I realize that although I wanted friends, I blocked myself from making them. I just was not ready to reach out. Every widow has her own time-table of grief, and I was still too shattered to muster that kind of energy.

As a psychologist, I know very well that if one is mourning a dearly beloved husband, joining a group will not bring him back or fill the emptiness in one's life. But it might help in other ways. I might have found a good friend among these women. You don't make friends by staying home watching television.

But, as I say, I blocked myself. I scorned widows in those early months. I did not want to have anything to do with widows. I shuddered at the idea of being a "professional widow," by which I mean a woman whose chief identification was as a widow. I resented the social discrimination that relegated widows to second-class citizenhood. The fact is that in the early months of my widowhood, I myself discriminated against widows. I thought I was different.

But this attitude changed. Little by little I became a "professional widow" to a certain extent without even realizing it. I discussed my widowhood on television and radio. I lectured about loss and loneliness. I cried quarts of public tears.

And I discovered the world of widows. There are nearly twelve million widows in this country. It is hard to believe that there are so many women just walking along the street or talking to you who have experienced the same turmoil of grief that you have. You learn that you are not an exception when for the first time a woman you consider both competent and controlled bursts into tears when she reminisces about her husband who died five years ago.

It is like being a member of a vast club. We have all shared the same initiation rites—the loss, the shock, the grieving, the loneliness. And it helps, it really does, to know that yours is not a peculiar and solitary case, to know that other women have felt lost and abandoned, that other women have talked to their dead husbands as if they were there, that other women have felt that life offers nothing more for them, that other women feel that they will never recover from their grief.

And you learn that you are not alone when incredibly another widow knows just what you need. I was sitting in the Beverly Hills Coffee Shop one morning, feeling forlorn, when two women who had watched me on KCBS called over to me, "Could we give you a hug?" They were widows, too. And a hug was just what I needed that morning.

Almost without my realizing it, the loneliness began to subside. There were times when life would be brighter for a day or two, for a week. And then, for no reason at all, it would be worse than ever. But the time came when there were slightly more ups than downs. I still cried. I was still lonely. I still missed Milt desperately. But life no longer seemed quite so black. There were still hours and days and weeks when I ached with loneliness, but it was not the cold, biting loneliness of the past.

Time helped soften my loneliness. I do not subscribe to the belief that "time heals all wounds," but the inevitable passage of time and the forward momentum of life do help. My great weapon against loneliness, however, was something Milt once told me. I cannot understand how I could have forgotten it, but I had until a year after Milt died when I woke up remembering how he had comforted me when my father died.

"He has not left you," Milt had said. "I believe that, even in death, people remain a part of their family. I believe that children carry with them a part of their parents' souls and consciousness. I believe that husbands and wives remain part of each other."

I lay there in bed thinking about what he had said, and I knew he was right. Milt *was* part of me, and if he was part of me, how could I be lonely? I cannot tell you how much this memory helped. I am not saying that I went from loneliness to happiness in a day, but from that time on everything began to get a little better.

Twelve

〜〜〜

I am not a timid woman, but after Milt died the world that I had always seen as full of promise suddenly became threatening. I developed a number of fears—some of them imaginary, others only too real. Most of it is behind me now, but there are still times when I feel lost and afraid.

Some of this unrest was due to what I think of as background clutter—unsettling and unpleasant, but not really important. This clutter was made up of little frustrations, feelings of incompetence, and an inner resistance to my new role as a widow and having to be responsible for everything.

Apart from those minor background worries and insecurities, I was haunted by money worries, by the absurd conviction that my grandson would disappear from my life now that Milt was gone, and by an acute fear for my physical safety. These fears colored my whole life.

I have told how I dissolved into tears when my sister asked me how to turn on the hot-water heater and I did not know how because Milt had always done it. A great deal of my insecurity revolved around having to do things that Milt had always done and fearing that I was not up to dealing with them. Ever since I was a little girl, I have prided myself on being competent and doing things well. Now I constantly worried that I was doing everything wrong.

Milt had always handled our insurance and taxes. Now I had to familiarize myself with these obligations as well as cope with the doctors' and hospital bills, the insurance forms, and the bills for the funeral expenses that came flooding in for six months after Milt died.

I found these tasks daunting. Not only were they hard to understand, they evoked graphic memories of Milt, ill and dying. I was often blinded by tears as I worked on them. There were late nights when I would get up from the desk where I had spent hours on a mountain of paperwork and pace the floor, crying and telling myself that I could never do it. Never! *Never!*

The interesting thing is that I had no such problems when it came to my own work. I could analyze book contracts, negotiate radio and television contracts, work out my professional expenses, handle my little office payroll, and all the rest—perfectly calmly and competently. It was just when it came to dealing with the matters Milt had always taken care of and the paperwork connected with his illness and death that I turned helpless.

But this was a case of temporary incompetence. This kind of thing, as I said, was just part of the background clutter. What really upset me—to the point of losing sleep over it—was my financial situation.

A few months after Milt died, I sold my car and started driving his red Porsche. It was a big mistake. Not only had I gotten rid of a perfectly good car with which I felt comfortable, but Milt's car was too powerful for me. Even so, I hung on to it, because I felt as if he were with me when I was behind the wheel. It was over a year before I finally realized I was being a little silly. I sold it and bought a less powerful, less expensive car. I could have afforded a better car, a more expensive car, but I felt financially insecure.

More than insecure. I felt poor. I spent hours worrying about money. I found myself sitting up in bed at night writing down lists of my expenses and my earnings to make sure I had enough money to get by.

If I lost out on a television show or a lecture was canceled, I thought of it in terms of both money and status lost. I worried that it spelled the end of my career. Even though on an intellectual level I knew this was not true, on an emotional level I saw myself starving in the gutter.

I had never worried about money before in my whole life, not even in the early years of our marriage when we were never sure if the peanut butter would last until payday. And once Milt became established in his practice and I in my career, we never had any money problems. In fact, we never lived up to our income. We did not have expensive tastes and lived modestly for people in our economic bracket. Our greatest extravagance was the farm, but we thought of it as an investment that Lisa and Amir and their children and their children's children would always have to enjoy.

I am fortunate in having been able to save enough money over the years that—barring some terrible worldwide catastrophe—I will always have enough to live comfortably. If I decided tomorrow never to do another lick of work—never give another lecture, never write another book, never do another television show, never take on another consulting project—I could manage very nicely.

And I knew this. But it did not stop me from worrying. I worried about every aspect of my financial situation. I worried because I learned that the old saying "Two can live as cheaply as one" was truer than I thought. Or, to put it another way, I learned that it costs almost as much for one to live as for two. My expenses had not decreased appreciably now that I was alone. I bought less food, but otherwise the household expenses were about the same. What was different was that now I had to meet all those expenses from my own earnings. And even though my income was sufficient to take care of them, I still worried.

I decided I had to cut down on expenses and that the sensible thing to do was sell the apartment. It was too big for one person, I told myself. I should move to a smaller place that would be less expensive to maintain. I did not stop to consider what I would do with all the files that fill my office and spill out into the guest bedroom. I did not think about where my secretaries would work if I moved into a little one-bedroom apartment. All I thought of was saving money.

Fortunately I was too busy with paperwork and too upset to do anything about it for several months, and when I finally had a breathing space, I was glad that I had not gotten around to selling the apartment. It is home. Milt and I lived here for years and years. The rooms are full of wonderful memories. It makes emotional sense for me to stay here. (This is just one more example of why a widow should not make any major decisions for at least a year after her husband's death. If I had sold the apartment, I would have regretted it bitterly.)

As a psychologist, I realize that insecurity was driving me. I had to be sure that if I did not have a husband to love and take care of me, I could at least count on having money to take care of me. Just knowing that I was financially secure was not enough. I had to keep reassuring myself over and over, making my lists, totting up income and outgo, until I reached the point in adjusting to life without Milt where I began to feel secure again.

Some of my financial concerns, however, were based on hard reality. I discovered how ready some people are to cheat a woman living alone.

My first encounter with one of these unscrupulous souls came when the water softener in my bathroom went on the fritz. I called the plumber. He puttered around, shook his head, and finally told me that it was a major repair. His estimate: $1,500. That was more than we had paid for the system in the first place. I told him I would let him know.

After he left I called the company that made the water softener. They sent out a man to look at it. He diagnosed the problem immediately. It needed a new thingamajig, and he took care of it on the spot. Total cost? Fifty dollars!

When I mentioned this to one widow, she told me that whenever she is quoted a price for work to be done around the house or the yard or for a car repair, she always says, "I'll have to ask my husband when he gets home tonight." And her "husband" almost always says the price is too high. "I make him sound like a terrible, penny-pinching ogre," she said, "and it always saves me money."

Another woman told me she protects herself by

getting three quotes on repairs and new appliances that cost over $100. "Under a hundred," she said, "I've found there's not much difference, but over a hundred . . . ! Well, it's a whole other ball game. Once I have the quotes, I tell them, I'll have to show them to my brother. I have no brother, you understand. Then I call them back and say my brother told me their quote was way too high. They usually come down ten to twelve percent."

Younger women may find these problems easier to deal with and not feel the need to call in an imaginary male, but many widows have never had to cope with these matters. Their husbands always handled them, and now they feel insecure—with good reason in many cases.

No matter how poor I felt, I had no real money worries, but for the majority of widows financial insecurity is a very real concern. So likely is it that a wife will one day be a widow (a good 60 percent of the women over sixty-five are widows) that sociologist Helena Lopata calls widowhood "the last stage in the role of wife."

And that last stage may find the wife poverty-stricken. More than a third of the American households that are headed by women (widowed, divorced, or single) are below the poverty level. One can look on the bright side and say that almost two-thirds of those households are above the poverty level, but one has to ask, Just how far above the poverty level? Fewer than 5 percent of all working women earn $35,000 or more a year. Women still earn one-third less than men on the average. It is safe to say that only a very small percentage of widows are as well off financially as they were when their husbands were alive.

If I, with my financial cushion, suffered from money fears, how must the young widow with two children feel when she discovers her husband had borrowed on his insurance to make the down payment on their now heavily mortgaged house? Or the widow in her seventies who learns that her husband's pension did not provide survivor benefits?

I received hundreds and hundreds of letters from widows after Milt died. Then I wrote an article for *People* magazine about what it felt like to have to start life all over again, and this prompted another avalanche of letters. Many of these women had sad stories to tell about their financial situations.

Take that woman whose husband had borrowed on his life insurance. He was only thirty-four, vigorous and healthy, when he was killed in a freak accident. They had two little boys, ages two and four. Her husband had not worked long enough at his last job to qualify for the company pension plan. He had borrowed the maximum on his insurance to make the down payment on their house. When he died, his widow was left with enough money to buy food and make the mortgage payments for six months. She sold the house for less than they paid for it and moved in with her in-laws.

"It is very difficult," she wrote. "I'm working as a receptionist and taking a computer programming course so I can get a better job. Someday I hope I can earn enough so the three of us can have our own home again. My in-laws live in an apartment, and there's no place for the boys to play outside. They don't know what hit them. And I don't know what hit me, either. I don't even have time to grieve, I'm so busy working and studying and taking care of the children. If he only knew what has happened to us . . . I don't know what I would have done without my in-laws. What if there was no one to stay with the children while I worked?"

The older widow, seventy-nine, wrote that she could not believe it when they told her that her late husband's pension stopped with his death. It did not provide survivor benefits. They had managed very well on his pension and Social Security. Now all she had was Social Security and the $5,000 in the savings bank they had earmarked for emergencies.

"Ben always said that I would not have to worry if something happened to him," she wrote. "He said that I'd be able to manage just fine on his pension and the Social Security. But it didn't work out that way. Now I'm living with my son and his wife. I give them my Social Security check, but sometimes she makes me feel as if I'm in her way."

I had many, many letters like these from widows, young and old, who found themselves in similar or worse financial straits. Money—the lack of it—is usually a widow's greatest problem. It exacerbates every other miserable aspect of her new life. Every prop is knocked out from under her at once. She loses her husband and her life-style—and often her home.

All married women should prepare themselves financially to be widows, no matter how old they are or how well off their husbands may be. Every married woman should ask herself, "If my husband were to die tomorrow, what would I have to live on?"

Few wives ever ask themselves this question. Few ever ask their husbands either, and when they do the answer may be something like "You don't have to worry, dear. There's insurance and my investments. You'll be fine." The older husband may reply, "You don't have to worry, dear. There's my pension and the insurance and Social Security and my stocks. You'll be fine."

Maybe. But there are questions a wife should ask. How much insurance do you have? Is it enough so the children and I won't have to sell the house? Enough to maintain our present life-style? And just what are those investments? Real estate? Stocks? Bonds? Certificates of deposit? What should I do about them if something happens to you? And where are they? In our safe-deposit box? Do you know if your pension pays survivor benefits? How much will I get? How much will I need?

These questions are only a beginning, a general guideline. Every family's situation is different. One of the most important things a wife should know is whether her husband has a will. She should also know where he keeps it and be familiar with its contents. Even in this age of enlightened feminism, there are wives, both young and old, who have no idea whether or not their husband has a will. If he does not, she should encourage him to make one.

I cannot pretend that Milt and I were models in this last respect. I have had a will ever since Lisa was a baby. My parents were lawyers and had impressed upon me the importance of having a will, but Milt never got around to making one until shortly before he died. He was not a worrier. I believe he thought he would live forever. Whenever I nagged him about making his will, he always promised he would—just as soon as he had time.

Well, he never had time until one day when Lisa was visiting him in the hospital and asked where his will was. When he said he did not have a will, she had him dictate one there and then and sign it, just so there would be something on paper. A week or two later when he was back home, a lawyer drew up a formal will for him based on what he had dictated to Lisa.

They say that money is not everything. I say that when you don't have any, it *is* everything. Widowhood is rotten enough without having to worry where the rent money or the mortgage payment is coming from.

I worried about money, but I was terror-stricken that I had lost my grandson. This was truly my most ridiculous fear, but it was very real to me. After Milt died, wherever I was, whatever I was doing, I felt that I was only half of what had been a whole—and that whole was lost forever. I feared that everyone I loved would drift away from me, because without Milt I was diminished as a person and there would be no love at all left in my life.

This particular fear started the day of the funeral. The service was over, and people were standing around the cemetery plot saying their good-byes to my mother and Lisa and me. Micah had obviously been very upset by the graveside ceremony. Raffi, his other grandfather, sensed that he needed to get away from that raw hole in the ground and asked if he would like to go for a walk. With obvious eagerness Micah nodded, and he and his grandfather disappeared down one of the paths in the cemetery.

At that point my heart went cold. I was sure that Micah would never feel close to me again now that Milt was dead. My firstborn grandchild was lost to me forever.

My fear seemed to be confirmed some weeks later when Lisa and her three little girls visited me in Florida. I love Lisa and my three granddaughters dearly, but Micah is special. My father had died. My husband had died. Now my grandson, the only male left who was blood of my blood, did not want to see me. He had told his mother he would rather stay home with his other grandparents. Micah, who loved the beach!

Even though I understood that coming to the house at Siesta Key—with all the memories it held of the good times he and his grandfather had enjoyed there—was too much for Micah just then, it was an especially bad time for me. I felt alone in the world.

I was convinced that since there was no man in my life, no one for Micah to be pals with, he would grow up away from me, except when Lisa insisted on duty visits. I know now that this pitiful, heart-breaking scenario would never have come true, but at that point it seemed as real as my grief.

Fortunately fate handed me an opportunity to rid myself of this fear. My work came to my rescue. I was asked to give a lecture in Alaska that summer. I immediately thought of Micah. What boy would not love a chance to explore Alaska? It would give me an opportunity to reestablish our relationship. After checking with Lisa and Amir to make sure that it was all right with them, I invited Micah to go to Alaska with me.

Once I had fulfilled my lecture obligation, the two of us spent a week traveling through the state. We were enchanted with Alaska's bears and moose, the

Dall sheep, elephant seals, and icebergs, the vast wilderness. We hovered over a glacier in a helicopter and were awed by the blue, blue ice. We saw bald eagles flying overhead, and Micah went on a dogsled ride. He went salmon fishing. We were fogbound for two nights on Kodiak Island, where we had gone in the hope—unfulfilled—of seeing some of the famous Kodiak bears. We met environmentalists and wildlife experts. Some bush pilots recognized me and invited us to join them for an evening. They told Micah stories of their harrowing adventures, and he was wide-eyed with excitement. It was a wonderful trip.

We talked about Milt occasionally, but always in happy ways. One night when we were looking at the stars, for instance, I told Micah that his grandfather had always wanted to look at the sky from the North and South Poles. And Micah reminisced about the New Year's Eve at the farm when Milt had taken him outside to show him the night sky through his big telescope.

By the end of the trip I no longer felt I had lost my grandson. Our shared experiences had strengthened the bond between us, and our relationship was as firm and loving as it had ever been. I will never be able to take Milt's place in Micah's life, but I have learned that I do not need to. There are other bonds between us, including our shared interest in new places and new ideas.

I also learned how very satisfactory it was to have

this chunk of time alone with my grandson. It really helped us become close. And I have started making time for each of the other grandchildren. Last spring Talya went to Paris with me. I had to attend a conference there, but the rest of the time was spent with my granddaughter. We breakfasted in sidewalk cafes and watched the world go by as we dipped our croissants in our hot chocolate. We went to the Louvre, where Talya decided to sketch the Mona Lisa. The Parisians were amazed by this child prodigy until they got a glimpse of the typical childish moon face she was drawing. I got to know her as I had never done before. When Lily and Ariel are old enough, I plan to take each of them on a special trip, too. And, of course, there will be other trips with Micah.

Although it had been nearly paralyzing, my fear of losing Micah was short-lived. In time I understood just how absurd it was, and I have become closer than ever to all four grandchildren, who are truly the joys of my life. And as I have slowly come to terms with life without Milt, I realize that it was truly silly of me to worry about money. But I still am concerned about my physical safety.

At first I was full of fears for my life. I did not go quite as far as looking under my bed at night, but every little noise when I was alone in the apartment made me jump. Especially the mysterious noise in the night. For months after Milt died, I was awakened at one o'clock every morning by a strange buzz that lasted for thirty seconds or so. I would get out of bed and prowl around the apartment looking for the source of the buzz. I could never find it. I worried that someone was trying to drill open the lock on the front door. Then I worried that one of the kitchen appliances was on the verge of exploding. There is probably nothing more irrational or terrifying than middle-of-the-night terrors.

Finally, months and months after Milt's death, when I stayed up well after midnight, packing up his clothes to send to Goodwill, I heard the buzz—practically in my ear. I was folding the sports jacket he had worn the last time I had taken him to the hospital, the time he never came home again. I searched through the pockets and found it. It was one of his watches, the kind that has a little alarm. I cannot imagine why he set it for one o'clock in the morning. That remains one of life's unsolved mysteries. But at least I knew what had caused that eerie buzz in the night. I kept the watch. I thought Micah might like to have it. But I turned off the alarm so that it would never scare me again.

I was frightened of being alone, because I felt unprotected. This was no imaginary fear. Celebrity has many rewards, but there are also drawbacks and dangers. Anyone who has a certain degree of celebrity—male or female, young or old—is right to be frightened. Think of John Lennon. Or think, as I did, of Rebecca Schaeffer, who starred in *My Sister Sam* and was killed by a fan the July after Milt died. Rebecca was not a great star like John Lennon, but she had achieved a certain success and was on her way to more. Prior to Rebecca's death, there had also been an attempt on the life of actress Theresa Saldana. Both episodes had received wide coverage in the media.

Shortly after these episodes, *USA Today* asked me to do an article on the deadly obsessive fan. In the course of investigating the research on the subject, I discovered that there is practically no celebrity who has not been either threatened or actually attacked. According to California psychiatrist Dr. Park Dietz, "there have been as many attacks on public figures by mentally disordered people between 1968 and 1989 as there were in the preceding 175 years."

The reason for the increase, I believe, is that years ago when people saw stars only on the big screen in the movie theater, they seemed very far away. And they shared their experience with hundreds of other people in the theater. The physical distance and the emotional dilution of sharing the experience were not conducive to an obsessional reaction. But today when a person is alone in his living room and watching an actress on TV or on a video, that actress is practically in his lap. From a psychological point of view, he owns that person.

The obsessive fan believes that this actress or celebrity that he adores has all the qualities he would like to have himself. His whole life begins to center about her (or him). He fantasizes situations in which they are together. He thinks about her constantly.

Most people have no need for this kind of fantasy. Other people—sometimes very normal people like a teenager, for instance, who is not ready to form a real relationship—fall in love with some actress from afar. They conjure up their own personal scripts with their own fantasies. It makes their lives more interesting and exciting. But they know that it is just a fantasy.

And then there are the seriously disturbed people—the deadly obsessive fans. They start to act out their fantasy scripts. They want to make them real. They want to be physically and emotionally close to this person whom up to now they have adored from afar.

What is wrong with adoring a person in this way? What is wrong with being adored in this way?

What is wrong is that it is dangerous.

The deadly obsessive fans are drawn to the halo of celebrity like moths to a flame. They want to meld with that person, be everything she or he is. The man who killed John Lennon wanted Lennon's celebrity to reflect on him. The man who stabbed Theresa Saldana thought of her as an angel and wanted her to take him to heaven with her.

The more I learned about the nature of the obsessive fan, the more it reinforced my feelings of in-

security and fear. Every celebrity gets a certain
amount of strange mail, mail that I have always handled by tossing it out. When Milt was alive, I never
gave it a second thought. Milt was there. He would
take care of me. But now I was scared. What if one
of these weird people zeroed in on me?

Added to this, my secretaries reported receiving
dozens of telephone calls and letters from men who
wanted to meet me after the article I wrote for *People*
magazine about starting life over as a widow. I am
willing to believe that ninety-nine percent of the
telephone calls and letters were absolutely sincere
from kind and thoughtful individuals, but what
about that other one percent?

My fears on this score came to a head the first
time I spent a night alone at the farm after Milt died.
It is a very safe place. We did have a burglary once,
and nothing terribly valuable was taken, nor was any
damage done to the house. Shortly afterward the burglars were caught, and everything they had taken was
returned to us. But on this night, I was so fearful
that I almost drove back to the city. The only thing
that stopped me was the knowledge that if I gave in
to my fear this time, it would be more difficult to
overcome. Once you run away from something, it
becomes very hard to stand and face it the next time.

So instead of fleeing, I went to the locked closet
where Milt kept his shotgun. He had always planned
to shoot the woodcock and ruffed grouse that were

seasonal visitors to our woods and fields, the idea being that I would then cook them. Fortunately that project never got off the ground. I planned to take the gun up to bed with me, and, I promised myself, if there were any prowlers, I would shoot to kill.

I took the shotgun out of its case and looked at it. It was larger than I had remembered. Holding it gingerly, the muzzle pointing straight ahead, I carried it upstairs and placed it on the bed. Then I went looking for bullets. Milt had kept them elsewhere, because he thought it a poor idea to have a gun and bullets in close proximity, especially with our grandchildren around so often. I found the small cardboard box of bullets and put them on the bed beside the gun.

I stood back and looked at them. I had never used a gun, and there was no instruction leaflet with it. Where did the bullets go? After a few minutes I decided that while it might be a good idea to have a gun for protection, this was not the gun for me.

Suppose someone did break into the house while I was asleep? The shotgun was so heavy that by the time I picked it up and pointed the right end at the intruder, anything might have happened. It was hardly the elegant little pistol one might keep on one's bedside table for midnight emergencies.

I left the unloaded shotgun on the floor beside my bed that night on the theory that no intruder would know that it was not loaded or that I had not the vaguest idea how to use it. The next morning I put it back in its case and locked it in the closet again. After that night, I did learn to use the gun safely and to feel secure with that knowledge.

That Monday I made an appointment with experts who installed some security devices at the farm, which they assured me would provide ample protection. This allayed one set of fears. The apartment house had its own security system, but I also had special security devices installed inside the apartment.

I still have a sense of uneasiness. I am careful now where I park the car. Are there plenty of people around? Is the place well lit? I am careful where I walk in the city, especially at night. I only go where there are people and good lighting. I carry very little money with me. I no longer open the door until I am sure that I know who rang the bell.

I have become so careful that when I went to the beach house in Florida this winter I did not even dare ask anyone to help me carry my suitcase in from the car. I had gotten there the night before Lisa and the children were scheduled to arrive, and my suitcase was just too heavy and unwieldy for me to get out of the car by myself. Normally I would have asked someone to help me, but it was the middle of the night and I realized that should I ask the strangers who lived on either side of me to help, it would be very clear that I was alone.

So I left the suitcase in the car and went to bed

that night without brushing my teeth or creaming my face—and without my pajamas. I realized then how terribly at risk a woman alone can be, when she does not even dare ask for help. Up until now I have always asked people to help me when I needed it. But I have come to realize that I cannot do that anymore. Not without increasing my vulnerability.

Recently when I had a flat tire, I did not get out and try to flag a passing car for help as I normally would have done. I locked the doors, turned on the flashers, and sat there until a state trooper came by and asked if I needed help. After that I got a car phone so that I could call for help myself if I ever had another flat.

When Milt was alive, I never gave a second's thought to obsessive fans, burglars, and all the rest. I never felt that I could possibly be in danger. Now I do. I know that this is sensible and that my fears are based on reality, but I resent having to be so careful.

I also know that I am not alone. Nor am I a special case. Every woman in a big city or not-so-big city is in a certain amount of danger. The single woman is in somewhat more danger than a married woman.

A woman does not have to be a big celebrity to attract the deadly obsessive fan. Although these people usually zero in on a person of prominence, that person may be prominent only in the obsessive fan's own world. She may be a teacher, a lawyer, the local beauty contest winner, or the very attractive mayor of the town.

My fear is accentuated because I am a widow and I have never before lived alone. Now I have to be responsible myself. I am proud that I have learned to be—but I still wish that I had never had to learn.

Thirteen

∽⚬∾

There is no rhyme or reason to grief. After all I have written about my yearning for Milt, my loneliness, my sense that life held nothing more for me—well, just nine months after Milt died, I had my first date.

Not only did I have my first date, I also began to realize that there were some advantages to life on my own. Contradictory as these two developments might seem, they were giant steps toward pulling myself out of the depths of grief. For the first time since Milt died, I was looking to the future.

There came a morning the September after Milt died when I woke up determined to get on with my life. I had been reading in bed the night before and come across some new statistics on longevity, including the fact that I now had a life expectancy of nearly twenty years more.

I started crying. Another twenty years of this life! Without Milt! How could I stand twenty more years of this anguished loneliness? The prospect appalled and frightened me.

In the morning things seemed brighter. If I had to live another score of years, I decided I might as well make the best of it. Indeed, I *should* make the best of it. Milt would have wanted me to. "You're alive, for God's sake," he would have said. "So live!" He had loved life, celebrated every minute of it. He was dead, but I still had the marvelous gift of life. I owed it to Milt not to waste it.

If I was to make the most of the rest of my life, I should get married again. I derive tremendous satisfaction from being able to help people by sharing my knowledge of psychology and human behavior, but my true métier is marriage. I had lived nearly forty years as a wife and had relished every day of it. I was born to be a wife, to love a man who loved me, pamper him, help him, share his life. Milt and I had pledged ourselves to each other for better or worse, and on every single one of our wedding anniversaries he used to kiss me and say, "I'm still waiting for the worse." Well, the "worse" came, of course. Worse? The worst! Death parted us. Nothing else could have. Milt would have remarried if I had died first. He was a man who luxuriated in marriage. He would approve if I remarried.

As I thought about it, I realized that I had a candidate for my next husband.

He called later that week. "We ought to get together," he said. "Would you like to go out for dinner some night?"

I had known Geoffrey for years, although not well. He had been a patient of Milt's, and his sons had gone to the same school Lisa had. His marriage had broken up, and he had moved out of the city and disappeared from our lives.

He called me after Milt's obituary appeared in *The New York Times*. He was very sympathetic, told me how much he had admired Milt as a man and as a physician and what a loss his death was. He said, as everyone does, "Be sure to let me know if there is anything I can do for you."

Well, of course there wasn't, but he called every now and then—"Just checking," he used to say. He would ask how I was doing, and we would chat for a few minutes. He told me about the waterfront condo he had bought in Connecticut and how he had taken up sailing. We exchanged anecdotes about our grandchildren. I told him about my problems with Milt's Porsche, and he sent me information about a couple of other makes of automobile that he thought would be more suitable for me. That kind of thing.

. . .

Now he was asking me to go out for dinner. His invitation threw me into a panic. It was one thing to speculate on the possibility that he might make a suitable husband and another to actually go out on a date with him. The only reason I had thought of him as a candidate was that he was the only man who had indicated any kind of interest in me whatsoever. It was like having someone call my bluff.

"Let me call you next week," I stalled. "I have a heavy schedule just now."

When I called him, I suggested that instead of our going out to dinner in the city, he might like to come to the farm for lunch on Sunday. "It's really beautiful there this time of year," I said. I warned that I would have to leave at four to catch a plane for Los Angeles.

"An afternoon in the country sounds great," he said. "I look forward to it."

This, I thought, was the best way to handle it. We could get to know each other a little, and since there was such a short time frame, there would be no possibility of it becoming too intimate or uncomfortable.

I told nobody about inviting Geoffrey to the farm, not even Lisa. I did not know how she would react, but I feared she might disapprove or feel that I was being disloyal to her father. I myself felt a bit guilty, almost as if I were cheating on Milt, asking another man to the farm. And I worried that the whole thing would be awkward.

I need not have worried. Geoffrey's role that Sunday was very much that of a friend of the family. Before lunch we went for a long walk through the fields and along the river, during which I discovered that I just did not know how to talk to a man. I make my living by talking, but this was different. All I could talk about was Milt. I found myself saying, "Milt and I used to . . . Milt always thought . . . Milt planned to . . . Milt liked to . . . Milt . . . Milt . . . Milt . . ."

Lunch—cheese soufflé, salad, and an apple pie with an old-fashioned butter crust that I had baked that morning—was less than successful. I had not realized he had to watch his cholesterol intake, and as I watched him pick at the soufflé and discard the rich flaky piecrust, I wished he had told me he was on a low-cholesterol regime.

But he could not have been kinder or more sensitive. When I mentioned that I hoped someday to marry again, he gave me some very wise advice. He said that I should be absolutely certain that when I found someone with whom I felt I could share my life, it was for the right reason. "For love," he said. "Don't fall into the trap of marrying just because you are lonely. You will be lonelier than ever. Marriage is not the magic cure-all. Love is what makes the difference.

"I learned this," he said, "from unhappy personal experience." He told me that he had lived with a woman for a couple of years after his divorce and it had not worked out. "We were both lonely," he said. "That brought us together. But it wasn't enough to keep us together.

"Love is a very rare commodity," he concluded. And I agreed with tears in my eyes.

He was stimulating and charming, but I was not sorry when it was time for him to leave. It had been an uneasy few hours for me—the first time in forty-three years I had spent significant time alone with any man except Milt. I waved good-bye, did the dishes, locked up the house, and left for the airport telling myself that it had been a mistake. There would never be another man for me, and that was that.

But it was not. All the way to the airport and during the flight to the West Coast and for most of the following week my head was swirling with "what ifs."

What if he should fall madly in love with me? I asked myself. He has a condo in Connecticut. He has three children. He has five grandchildren.

If we were to marry and I were to move into his house, I would never feel that it was really my home. Besides, it would probably be too small. We would have to get a new house. But I liked my apartment. I did not want to live somewhere else.

But what if we did find a new house that we both liked? My things might not fit into it, or he might not like them and I would have to put them in storage. And there might not be room for me to have an office at home. And what if he did not like having my secretaries in the house all day long?

He liked living in Connecticut. That would mean I would have to spend hours and hours commuting back and forth to New York. And what if my secretaries did not want to commute? If they did commute, would there be room in the driveway for their cars?

What if he should resent my constant traveling? It was part and parcel of my work—the lectures, the television on the West Coast, the seminars and consultations.

What if he wanted me to give up my work? I could not possibly give up my work. It was too important a part of my life. And besides, I had contractual commitments for the next two and three years.

What if he wanted to spend weekends on his boat? I hated sailing. I would be bored stiff.

What if his children did not like me? That would be a heavy burden for both of us. And what if Lisa did not like him? Or he did not like Lisa? What would I do? My daughter and her husband and my grandchildren—they meant so much to me. I could not bear it if they resented my new husband or felt uncomfortable in our house.

And that low-cholesterol diet of his!

I went so far as to buy a low-cholesterol cookbook. I had thought I really should ask him back again and cook him a low-cholesterol meal as an apology for having clogged up his arteries with the cheese soufflé and apple pie, but the more I looked at the recipes, the less they appealed to me. Cholesterol, I told my-self, is what God put in food to make it taste good. And since my cholesterol level is low, I don't have to worry about it. If Geoffrey and I were to get mar-ried, I would have to cook two dinners every night— one for him and one for me. I enjoy food too much to give up beef and butter and eggs and cream when I don't have to.

What if he should call again and repeat his dinner invitation? Did I want to accept it?

What if I told him I preferred staying home and invited him to have dinner with me at home? What if he construed this as a tacit invitation for a sexual overture?

And what if he did? Could I ever feel comfortable with another man? My body is not that bad, but it's not what it used to be. With Milt, it did not matter. Our bodies had grown old together. We never noticed each other's slight imperfections.

That is one of the wonderful things about a happy marriage. When a man sees an old girlfriend for the first time in twenty years, he thinks to himself, She has really aged. But the same twenty years makes no change in his perception of his wife's looks.

The image your husband carries of you in his heart and his mind's eye is that of the young woman he fell in love with ten, thirty, fifty years ago. Despite the extra pudge around your middle, the little droop here and sag there, he still sees you the way you looked when he fell in love.

There are two reasons for this: first, because it has been a gradual change, and second, because he will not allow himself to be conscious of the change. His inner censor helps him overlook the droopy bosom and the second chin. No wonder they say love is blind.

But a man seeing you naked for the first time— ah, that has to be different. Especially if the man has been on sexually active terms with a younger woman, as Geoffrey had been. I would worry that he was comparing my body to that of the younger woman—and finding it wanting.

I felt like such an idiot with all these thoughts going through my mind, especially since nothing had been done or said to make me believe that I would actually have to confront any of these "what if" situations. But that was exactly the way my mind was working. The result of all my worrying and self-probing was that I decided that Geoffrey was not for me. Even if most of my "what ifs" turned out to be baseless, I had no feeling for him that would impel me to change my life enough so that I could share it with him.

I did not realize it at the time—in fact, I was rather perturbed at what I saw as extravagant worries about situations that did not and probably never would exist—but these "what ifs" were part of a learning process, learning about myself and what I wanted.

People often forget that the widow is undergoing a series of personal and emotional changes during her mourning. She is not the same woman she was before her husband died. How could she be? So much in her life has changed.

Psychologists often speak of the "ripple effect" to demonstrate the far-reaching effect of the smallest change in one's life. As with a pebble tossed in a pond, the ripples of change spread to the very edge of the pond, to the very limits of one's personality. A widow experiences many, many changes, and most of them are major. She has to get to know her new self, and asking "what if" when confronted with the need for decisions can help her do this.

I would advise every woman—single, divorced, or widowed—who is considering marriage to put herself through a series of similar "what ifs." I was surprised at what I learned about myself.

One might think that I had learned a lesson from this—that I was not ready for another man in my life yet, that I was not even ready to start dating a man. But a few weeks later when I was in Los Angeles, I called a man who had written me after reading the article in *People* magazine. He had asked me to have dinner with him when I was in Los Angeles.

He was a stranger, but I knew his name. He was prominent in the film world, an attorney and an independent producer, and as far as I knew, he was not married. He had written a wonderful letter full of sympathy and admiration for my "bravery" and "courage" in facing Milt's death.

I had put the letter aside but done nothing about it. Now I thought, Why not? I called and I told him I was alone in the city and would like to invite him for dinner the following night. I made a point of emphasizing that it was *my* invitation. I wanted to be in control of the situation.

He said he would love to have dinner with me. He was just delightful, very bright and extremely talented. Our dinner date was fun. We went to Chasen's, and a lot of people who knew him came over to our table to say hello, and a lot of people who knew me came over, so it was like a little party. I could see that life with him would be stimulating and that we would have a lot in common. Like me, he was a very hard worker. He told me he had never married because he had always been too busy. "But the time is coming," he said, "when I will want to put down roots."

When I got back to the hotel that night my "what ifs" started up again. What if *he* were to fall madly in love with me?

Could I sell everything I had to move to the West Coast? It would mean tearing up all my roots. It came down to a matter of energy. Did I have the energy to make a whole new life?

And what if he wanted children? If he married, he would undoubtedly want children, and I could not give him children.

No, I was not for him, and he was not for me. My reaction? Relief.

So there I was, back to square one. I had flirted with the idea of dating and marriage but come nowhere near doing either, not even of establishing a friendship or a relationship. But I had tried. It had taken more courage than I had thought to have these dates. And it had been rather depressing to realize that neither of these men had been particularly interested in me. Nor I in them. But the experience had been useful.

I learned that I may have been ready to think of marriage, but I was not ready for marriage itself. As Geoffrey had realized when I told him I eventually wanted to remarry, I was not seeking love, nor was I ready to give love, nor was sex an element in my desire to remarry.

My sex drive had shut down like a furnace in July. I was no more interested in sex than I was in learning to hang-glide. Most widows lose interest in sex for months, often for a year or more after their husband's death. Sex takes energy, and grief, with its debilitating emotional strain, is physically draining. The widow usually has all she can do to drag herself through her daily routine. Sex is the last thing on her mind.

But what about those women who plunge into a steamy sexual relationship a few short weeks after the funeral? A few of them have a very strong sex drive that refuses to be suppressed. With others sex may be a way of getting rid of the anger they feel at being left alone in the world.

Some women enter into sexual relationships within a few months of their husband's death in a desperate search for a husband. They want to get their lives back on an even keel again. They want to be part of a couple once more. If they can only get married again, they think, life will resume its happy normalcy. For them sex is both a bait and a short-cut to getting to know a man.

But the majority of widows who have sex within months of their husband's death go to bed with a man, not because they want it or feel like it, but just to be close to someone, to be able to snuggle up to a warm body in bed. There comes a time when a widow is so anxious not to be alone in her empty house or apartment that she trades sex for companionship.

It is like walking the dog. You want a dog, but you do not particularly enjoy walking it. But since you really want the dog, you walk it. The same holds true for the widow. She is not really interested in sex, but since she does not want to be lonely, she engages in sex. This may provide momentary comfort, but usually it turns out to be a basically disappointing exercise and leaves her lonelier than ever.

Sometimes widows have sex simply because they don't know how to say no. Many men, particularly married men, think the widow is sitting around panting for a man to relieve her sexual tensions, and they make sexual overtures almost as if they were doing her a favor.

Women often have trouble dealing with this, especially when the couple are friends. They do not want to antagonize the husband and, as a result, face the end of the friendship. Especially when they are feeling so alone. It is possible to say no without jeopardizing the friendship. Usually it can be done very gently, since the man is never as sure of himself as he may seem. Sometimes a sad smile and a shake of the head will get the message across that you are touched that he is so concerned for you, but that your grief is just too raw for you to even consider sex.

It takes time for a widow to adjust to the idea of sex and intimacy with another man, to a sexual relationship based on love and nurturing, a relationship that can lead to marriage. Most widows have to work through their grief and come to terms with life without their husband before they can become seriously and lovingly involved with another man.

I had not reached that point yet. What I had been

seeking was a surcease of loneliness. And marriage could not give me that. Not yet.

Will I ever remarry? I don't know. Right now I doubt it. I do not even know if I really want to. What I do know is that the odds are against me—against almost every widow. And one reason for this is that the average woman is fifty-six years old when her husband dies. And that really narrows the field.

The wealthier and more prominent a man is, the younger a wife he wants. The second wife is usually "a decade or two younger than her husband," reported *Fortune* magazine in an article on top executives' second wives. She is "sometimes several inches taller, beautiful, and very often accomplished. The second wife certifies her husband's status and, if possible, given the material she has to work with, dispels the notion that men peak sexually at age eighteen. Powerful men . . . demand trophy wives."

In other words, marriage is what psychologists call a "social exchange," an equation in which $a + b = x + y$. Take an example in which a = wealth, b = status, x = ambition, and y = intelligence. This might describe the marriage of a woman of wealth and social standing to a lawyer ten years younger than herself, a man who she is convinced will one day be at the top of his profession. To the lawyer, his spouse's wealth and social level are strong enough assets to cancel out her age. To his wife, his intelligence and potential are strong enough assets to cancel out his present impecunious state. Each is convinced that it is an "even Steven" exchange.

Widows usually have little to offer in the way of social exchange. For instance, let a = a sixty-year-old widow with a limited income and a desire to travel, and b = pleasant looks and a dumpy figure, and let x = a sixty-year-old divorced business executive with a desire for a sophisticated life-style, including travel, and y = good looks, although slightly bald. It may seem like a fair exchange, but when you examine it in the light of reality, it is not.

The executive will end up marrying an attractive younger woman who, he believes, will fit in with the new life-style he desires. The younger woman will feel there is a fair exchange of assets since he has the money to give her the life-style she covets. And the widow will stand alone.

Or match that widow with a sixty-five-year-old widower with a generous retirement income and a strong desire to get remarried and once again enjoy the comforts of a well-run home. This might seem like an equal social exchange, but the widower too will almost always choose a younger woman. Why? Because he will feel more in control if his wife is younger; because younger women tend to be more attractive than older women; because he wants his second wife to outlive him and be able to take care of him if he should fall ill; and because he can pick and choose.

There are far more available marriageable women than men. There are some twelve million widows in this country and fewer than three million widowers. So when you add the divorcées and single women to this pool of availability, most widowers have a wide choice.

The young widow has a better chance than the older woman. She has more to offer—youth, possibly beauty, charm, a greater sexual drive. And in the early 1990s, she has demographics on her side. There is a slight—and rare—shortage of young women in this country. According to the Census Bureau, there are some 2.3 million more unmarried men in their twenties than women. Nevertheless the young widow's prospects of marriage are not as good as those of a single woman of the same age. A prospective suitor may shy away from having to help bring up another man's children. Or he may feel that the expense of raising her children may limit the number of children of his own that he can have with her. Some men will not want to start marriage with a couple of young children underfoot.

When I look at the facts of second marriages in this way, I understand that my chances of remarrying are slim. However, I have discovered that as the months pass, I am less and less willing to give up the freedom I have—freedom that I never wanted but, now that I have it, would find hard to relinquish. I have found there are advantages to the single life. And I am not alone in this discovery.

There is an astonishing number of widows, young and old, who have decided that although their marriages were happy and rewarding, they do not want to remarry.

One woman who had been married for twenty-two years said it came as a shock to her when three years after her husband's death, she realized that "I did not want to marry again. It wasn't that I was comparing everyone to my late husband and none of them measured up, but that I simply did not want to be tied to anyone. I am free as a bird, and I intend to stay that way."

Another widow said, "I discovered a new freedom after my husband died and a whole new sense of self. I'll never get married again." There is a man who is very much a fixture in her life, but she has ruled out marrying him. "I travel with him. We are invited to the same parties. We enjoy the same things, but I am fifty-eight, and marriage would not give me anything I need. I like my life just as it is."

A twenty-eight-year-old whose husband died four years ago leaving her with a six-month-old baby barely manages to support herself and her son with her insurance, Social Security payments, and part-time jobs. It has not been easy, but when I asked if she wanted to get married again, she shrugged. "I've gotten so used to being on my own that marriage would be a tough adjustment at this point."

When I asked a very attractive woman, a former model, if she thought she might remarry, she said, "I'm forty-nine, and that's old enough to know that it is impossible to say what tomorrow will bring, but I think that for me remarriage would be a mistake. I find the life of a single woman very rewarding. I've never felt so alive in my life."

Older widows seem even more set against remarriage than the younger women. They do not want to go through the process of adjusting to life with another individual, nor do they want to go through the agony of nursing another man through a terminal illness.

A fifty-eight-year-old widow who had recently turned down a marriage proposal said, "I've known him almost all my life, and I like him; but he is twelve years older than I am, and he'll probably die before I do. I nursed my husband through a long illness. I can't go through that again.

"I thought seriously about his proposal because I am lonely and it would be nice to have a man around the house again. But it would also be a lot of bother. Meals to plan, his laundry to do, having him underfoot all the time.

"He needs me more than I need him. He needs me

to provide a home and all the services that make a home comfortable. All I need him for is to keep me from being lonely. As it is, he is a good friend. And that's enough," she concluded firmly.

"It is still the usual pattern to marry an older man, and with age, the chances of illness increase," said a woman in her late sixties. "I don't want to spend the rest of my life as a nurse. It was different with my husband. We had been married thirty-five years. We had shared more than half our lives. I wanted to take care of him and be there for him. I could never feel the same about another man."

These women are by no means exceptions. A survey of 390 Chicago widows found that only 80 wanted to get married again. When asked why not, their answers were remarkably similar: "I'm free and independent" was the refrain.

Very few of the widows I have talked with in the last two years have mentioned sex as a reason to remarry. This bears out what the research team headed by Dr. Victor Malatesta of the University of Pennsylvania School of Medicine discovered when they asked widows how they felt about no longer having sex in their lives. The widows were divided into five age groups—fourties, fifties, sixties, seventies, and eighties. Only the youngest group reported missing the sexual aspect of marriage acutely.

The era of the so-called merry widow seems to be over—if it ever existed. AIDS and other sexually transmitted diseases like herpes have put an end to the freedom of the sexual revolution. Women are no longer willing to trust their bodies to casual acquaintances.

"They lie to you," one young woman said. "They think that if you are a widow, you're just dying to hop into bed with them. But even if I am, I won't. There's too much at stake. Maybe . . . sometime . . . if there is a man who I think is really serious about me . . . and if I've known him for a while . . . and if we've talked about this . . . well, then," she concluded, "I guess I would. But I'd let him know that marriage was on my mind. Not just sex."

I have to admit that the idea of having a lover has crossed my mind. After my abortive experiences with the men I described, I thought that perhaps what I really wanted was a man who would be there as a companion and a lover, but not as a husband. Just someone to banish the loneliness. What it boiled down to was that I wanted a man in my life, but not in my house.

If this had been fifteen years earlier, perhaps a lover would have been the solution for me, given my unwillingness to give up my home and my way of life. But like that young widow, I am not willing to take the chance. A man who is that available may have had a very promiscuous past. And besides, once I thought it out, I decided that it was one of those things you think about—but never do.

. . .

After all I have written about my fears and insecurities and sense of vulnerability, I almost hesitate
to report my next effort to fill the void in my life. It
was truly an idiotic thing to do, but I did it.

One lonely night I was sitting up in bed reading
magazines. I leafed through the personal advertising
columns of *New York* magazine, reading ads like
"College grad, forties, wants meet thirtyish woman
to share long walks, country dinners, good music"
and "Woman exec., attractive, seeks man in fifties
interested in theater, travel, French restaurants, and
long-term relationship."

There were two ads by men in their sixties. Both
were looking for a mature woman and a long-term
relationship. I answered both. A few weeks later a
man called.

"Are you the real Dr. Joyce Brothers?" he
asked. "Yes," I told him. "I am."

"And did you answer an ad in *New York* magazine?"

"Yes," I replied. "I did."

"You know," he said, "I have a ten-dollar bet with
my psychiatrist. He said he was sure you were not
the real Dr. Brothers."

"Well, good. You win your bet."

There was a short silence, and then he said, "Well,
good-bye."

I was a little startled. I did not think that I would
be interested in this man, but I had not expected a

brush-off. "Would you like to meet for coffee some-time?" I asked him.

There was another short silence. "Umm," he finally said, "I'll have to think about that," and hung up.

What would I have done if he had agreed to meet me for coffee?

It was within the realm of possibility that he could have turned into one of those deadly obsessive fans that I described in the previous chapter. He was probably a very decent and lonely man, but maybe not. Who knows?

Nothing happened to me—except rejection, of course. But it was a terribly foolish and rather dangerous thing to do. I hope that by spelling out just how foolish I was, other women will realize the inherent dangers in this kind of meeting.

Becoming a widow is a change of the first magnitude, and it shakes your whole life to its very foundations. I can look back and see that I was working my way out of my grief, although it was often one step forward and two steps back. I was beginning to accept some of those changes—no longer raging against the malign fate that had torn the happy fabric of my life, but starting a life of my own, even though some of my attempts were dangerously foolish.

I was beginning to think of the pros and cons. Should I marry? Or not? Should I take a lover if one should offer himself? Or not? What was it in life that

I valued now? Little by little I began to make a new life for myself.

In fact, as I thought about all my "what ifs," it was obvious that I really did not want to change my life in any way. I did not want to move. I did not want to change my work habits. I did not want to accommodate to another person's life-style. All I wanted was to escape my loneliness. And marriage was not the answer. At least, not yet.

But I have not closed the door on the possibility. Who knows what the future might bring? I read something when I was researching loneliness that stuck in my mind. Dr. Robert Weiss, the sociologist who has been called the father of loneliness research, wrote that the right man can be the most effective cure for loneliness.

When a woman forms a new meaningful attachment, he said, her loneliness vanishes as if by magic. "Her body tone changes, her self-image changes, her energy level changes. It is as though she had taken a powerful pill."

If that right man should come along . . . ? I do not know. It almost seems too much to hope for. If he did, I think I would be a little frightened. A little shaky. A little incredulous. And so very happy. I suspect I would tell myself that Milt had sent him to me.

Fourteen

❦

Widows often describe themselves as broken up or shattered after their husband's death. "I felt like a deck of cards that was thrown up in the air," said one woman. "It has been a struggle to put everything back together."

I felt much the same. Milt had a sculpture that looked something like a globe that had exploded into little pieces. Each fragment was on the end of a wire and would tremble in the slightest current of air. I felt like that sculpture for the longest time—a sad Humpty Dumpty of a woman. Milt had been the half that fitted into my half to make a whole. With his death, that whole had exploded into little fragments that could never be put together again.

I was positive that I would never feel whole again.

I would have sworn to it. But after a year and a half I have come to realize that I *am* a whole. As the months go by I feel more and more together, so much so that I feel like a different woman.

On the anniversary of his funeral, I had a one-sided bedtime conversation with Milt. I told him that it looked as if I was never going to marry again, because I did not think I could ever find anyone who would be right for me. But that was all right, I told him. I was getting comfortable with the idea of being a widow and living alone. I had adjusted to coming home to an empty apartment. I had lived without him for a year, and I knew that this was the way it was going to be. My work and the family would be satisfying enough, I assured him.

If I were to have that conversation with him today, six months later, I would have to say that while I am quite comfortable living alone, I worry that this might be the way it is going to be for the rest of my life. Work and family are fine, I would tell him, but the truth is that I am longing to find a good and kind man and get married again. I am not quite ready yet, I would tell him, because you are still too important in my life, but I know this will change. It is changing.

I suspect Milt would respond, "It's about time you got your act together. You ought to be married. Just make sure he's a really good man."

. . .

That January night, I lay there for a while and thought about what I had told Milt. And I looked back. Six months, nine months, twelve months. I had come a long way from that brutally cold winter morning a year before when I had dropped those few grains of earth onto his coffin, a long way from that numb woman who had no idea what lay before her.

It was a strange night—a kind of an emotional stock taking. It had been a hard year, a terrible year, but I had survived. I was still lonely, but not all the time. I still cried, but less and less. I still said "our." I still said "we." When I corrected myself and substituted "my" and "I," I felt a bit uncomfortable— as if I were being self-centered. I still compared every man I met with Milt, and of course none of them measured up.

Most of me was still looking backward, but a very important part was looking ahead to the unknown, to the future. I still could not envision the future except in terms of the past. My life with Milt had been so utterly satisfactory, I could not imagine any other kind of life. But I knew there was something new and different out there, and I was almost ready for it.

That night, for the first time, I was sure that there would come a time when I would no longer walk in the shadow of loneliness and depression. That "conversation" with Milt was a major milestone on my way out of the tunnel of grief. I do not mean that life was all sunshine and roses after that, but it was the beginning of a number of long steps forward.

I knew there would be no future for me until I could let go of Milt. And that was proving difficult.

From the very beginning I dreamed about him. At first he was always angry with me, but I did not care. It was wonderful to have him with me for those few minutes, no matter how disagreeable he was. I always knew it was a dream. And when the dream faded, I woke up and cried.

By that autumn my dreams had begun to change. One night he was with me, no longer ravaged by cancer, no longer bone thin and drawn, no longer angry, but his old self again. The angry Milt reappeared occasionally after that, but more and more often my dreams were of Milt as he was before his illness.

When the time came that he was no longer angry with me in my dreams, I knew I had put a small part of my grief behind me. I had dealt with his anger at cancer and impending death.

In the last months of his life, I had been the target of his anger. He had no one else to get angry with. He knew that no matter what he said, I would always be there for him. I knew that he had to get rid of his anger somehow, and I was willing to be the lightning rod. I had resolved never to show that his anger got to me, but it had. And it took all those months before the angry Milt finally disappeared from my dreams and I was able to recover from my role as lightning rod.

Absorbing another person's anger, especially the anger of the man you love, can be very hard on a woman. Dr. James Coyne, a psychologist at the University of Michigan, studied a group of women who "tried to keep their husbands from getting upset by hiding their own anger or by giving in, instead of having an argument." He found that "this made the husbands feel more self-confident, but a third of the wives became so depressed and anxious that they needed therapy." I had not needed therapy, but my acceptance of Milt's anger took a lot out of me and resulted in those dreams of my angry husband for months after his death.

The second spring after he died, I had what I think of now as the "miracle dream." We were at the farm, just the two of us. It was snowing hard. The house was toasty warm, a fire blazing on the hearth. There was the spicy fragrance of the fresh-baked gingerbread that I had just taken out of the oven.

Suddenly Milt and I were outdoors. The snow had stopped. The sun was bright. We were slipping and sliding on the snow as we made our way down the hill toward the brook. We were holding hands and laughing. And everywhere there were flowers. Daffodils were blooming on low woody bushes. The trees were in bloom with roses and daisies. It was a fantasy land. We picked some of the flowers to put on the dinner table that night.

As we went back to the house, our arms full of flowers, I told Milt, "How lovely it is to have a second chance to be with you." I totally appreciated what it meant to be with him. It was a wonderful feeling. I knew it was a dream, but even when I woke up, the feeling of pleasure and closeness persisted.

I have never had such a beautiful dream again, but Milt is still with me in my dreams. One of my recent dreams was that we were at the farm with his friend Donald. And there was a new place—a romantic ruin—that we wanted to explore. We prowled through the wreck of an old stone house and wondered who had lived there and why it had been allowed to fall into such decay.

Then I said, "Let's get the farm ready for the summer, since we only have this one time to be together." And the three of us went to work taking the chairs out of the cellar and putting up the hammock and painting the porch screens, picking up the branches that had fallen during the winter, and generally getting spruced up for summer. The place looked wonderful when we finished. I only wish it looked as good in the real world as it did in my dream world.

There are still many things that I want to ask Milt. Just trivial things like "Where did you put such and such?" or "How should I do this or that?" Now, in my dreams, I ask him these questions. I get no answers, but once I have asked my question, that little niggling concern, whatever it was, is put to rest.

One can analyze dreams like these to a fare-thee-well and draw all sorts of conclusions. I am content simply to accept them. I know, even in the middle of these dreams, that Milt is only lent to me. I know very well that all these questions I feel I must ask Milt are simply a way of hanging on to him. I also know that little by little I am learning to get along without him—and that one day I will not have any more questions. I do not expect my Milt dreams to last much longer, but right now each one of them is like a gift, a rerun of the happy days I miss so much.

Dreams seem to be turning points for many widows. Two woman, both widows of celebrity husbands—Judy Belushi and Sally Burton—told me of having experienced dreams in which they were confronted by angry husbands. As in my case, these dreams of anger were replaced within a year by calmer, more realistic dreams in which their husbands were more loving, more themselves. One woman shared a dream with me that she said had helped her get on with her life again. She dreamed it was summer and she was sitting on a rocking chair on the porch. She saw her husband coming up the front walk, and she ran down the porch steps to meet him. "Where have you been?" she asked, and threw her arms around him. But there was nothing there.

"I knew it was Jim," she told me, "I knew he was there, but when I hugged him, there was nothing.

"I cried when I woke up, but in a way I was happy. He had come back to see me. After that I began to think that he would not like to have me moping around all the time, that I should try to pull myself together and get on with life. And that is exactly what I did."

Different women have different turning points. Author Monica Dickens wrote that she was driving home and thought of all the times when her husband was ill and dying that she had driven too fast on that road, because she'd wanted to get home to him. Then she realized, "Now I was free not to worry. . . . I had been given a devastating loss, but I'd also been given freedom. I'd better use it."

I am having other milestone experiences, which I see as signs of recovery. Some of them are quite silly. For instance, Milt and I occasionally used to watch horror movies in bed at night. I would move over to his side and snuggle up when the horror got too horrible. He was always amused when I grabbed for his hand at especially scary moments.

After he died, horror movies were just too terrifying for me to watch alone. One night I had been working all evening and I wanted to see something relaxing before I went to sleep. The title of one film being shown on television that night suggested it was a comedy, but it turned out to be a horror movie, and I had to turn it off after ten minutes. I was so scared that I did not dare get out of bed and go to the kitchen for the glass of milk I wanted before going to sleep. Who knew what horrors might be lurking in the dark beyond the bedroom door?

Two months later, when there was nothing I really wanted to watch, I decided to risk a horror movie. And I was able to go to the kitchen afterward and do the dishes without batting an eyelash. This may seem trivial, but to me it meant that in the course of those two months I had become a little more self-reliant, a little braver.

It is hard to get rid of some things, to decide what should be kept as remembrances and what should be thrown or given away. I heard about a widow who treasured the core of the apple her husband ate the afternoon before he died. It was months and months before she could bring herself to throw away its desiccated remains. When she did, she was extremely relieved.

"I hated having that thing around," she said, "but I felt guilty about throwing it out. It was as if I would be throwing his memory out. But I finally decided that it was not a memory, just a dried-up apple core."

One woman had treasured the tape from their answering machine. "It had his voice on it. It is the only thing I have with his voice. I could not use it on the machine after he died. I bought another one to replace it. But every once in a while I'd put it back in the machine just to hear his voice one more time.

"The tape finally broke. I felt bad, but by that time I knew I could not keep playing it over and over. What good did it do?"

That is the question the widow must ask herself when it comes to sorting out what she should keep and what she should go. These are heart-wrenching decisions. There are other decisions that are even more difficult. For instance, how long should a widow continue to wear her wedding ring? This particular decision was made for me—temporarily, at least—on the day of Milt's funeral. One of the diamonds fell out of the ring, probably at the cemetery. I like to think it fell into his grave. I did not notice the loss until I went to bed that night.

The ring is at the jeweler's, where it has been for the last eighteen months. The diamond has been replaced, but I still have not gone back to get the ring.

When I do, I don't know whether I will wear it. At first there was no question in my mind. Of course I would wear it. I had worn it for thirty-nine years. I felt lost without it. It was practically part of me. But now? Now I am not sure whether I want to put the ring back on my finger.

How long does a marriage last? The vows are "until death do us part." Death has parted us. Would it be a sign of love and loyalty to continue wearing the ring? Or would it be a sign that I was not able to accept Milt's death, that my life is still centered on him?

I wonder if a wedding ring would discourage some man I might meet in the future—even though he knew I was a widow. Would he feel I was still too involved with my late husband? This situation may never arise, but I admit I have thought about it.

The farm may turn out to be another one of the hard decisions I will have to make. Should I keep it or not? I can hardly believe it, but I do not enjoy going to the farm as much as I used to.

Without Milt, I wander around the house and the fields, not really settling down to anything. The herb garden that I was so proud of has gone wild. The thyme has spread far beyond its borders. And the rosemary was winter-killed because I forgot to dig it up and bring it inside last fall. Perhaps I had a subconscious need to forget. Rosemary is for remembrance, and the farm is too full of memories as it is.

I used to think I would spend every weekend there, but there is no joy in it for me any longer. I go there less and less. Since Thanksgiving I have only gone there once a month, and then just to check on things with the foreman. I rarely stay more than a few hours.

I don't think the farm will ever be the source of solace and peace for me that it was for the two of us. Now it is just an obligation. I no longer feel it is part of my life.

This situation may change. I am certainly not going to sell it now. That would be a truly major decision, and I do not feel up to it yet. Lisa and her family love the farm, but they live a thousand miles away. Milt and I always planned to leave the farm to them, but I wonder now whether they would find it a joy or a burden.

Another milestone has been my recent ability to accept that Milt, like every other human being, had faults. There are times when I am relieved that I am living alone. Milt was an impatient man. He had very little tolerance for stupidity or carelessness.

Once Lisa and I were out shopping. The two of us got out of the car and automatically locked and closed the doors—and immediately realized we had locked the keys inside the car. We agreed—without the need for words—that we were never going to tell Daddy. We knew that if push came to shove, Milt had a key and would come rescue us. But I called the police and they were able to open the door, and we never told because we knew he would ask how two so-called intelligent people could be so god-damned stupid. And if we had had to ask him to come rescue us with his key, we would never have heard the end of it.

If I ever lock my keys inside of the car again, I won't turn a hair. No one will tell me how stupid I was. I won't have to feel guilty. If I make a mistake, I won't have to confess that I did something dumb.

It is liberating to know that I am the only one I have to answer to.

This makes Milt sound like a monster and an ogre who terrorized his wife and daughter. He was nothing of the sort. He was a softie who would do anything for us, but he was impatient.

During this second year, I have become more accepting of the changes in my life. I actually welcome them. Most of the first year, the days were endless. It was the first time in my life that time seemed to drag. I had this awful sense of being on a treadmill to nowhere. And I did not care. Nothing seemed to matter.

All that has changed. And I have changed as well. I should put it even more strongly. I feel transformed. I am more interested in people and much more sensitive to them. I have started looking out beyond my personal horizon, and I am broadening my professional horizon in an effort to leave the world a little bit better if I possibly can.

When Milt was alive, I made a point of keeping our time together free from my work. I was usually away from home one or two nights a week, but when I was home I was completely Milt's. It was his time.

In order to do that, I had to make the most of my time alone. I never got on a plane without a huge carry-on bag full of reading—magazines, newspapers, professional journals, my mail. I would sit there on transcontinental flights—reading, tearing out things to bring home for my secretaries to file, making notes for future lectures, writing my column.

I was always aware that someone was sitting on the next seat, but I could never have told you whether it was a man or a woman or a three-headed alligator, because I was concentrating so hard. If that person tried to strike up a conversation, I would always apologize and say that I had a tremendous amount of work to do on the flight.

I also tended to avoid casual conversations with people. I rarely took time to say good morning in the elevator or exchange a few words about the weather. I was always in a hurry to get someplace.

All that has changed. Milt's death has given me the luxury of time. I am doing more and working harder than I used to, but I have more free time. My evenings and my weekends are free now, and I no longer fear their emptiness. Now I look forward to them. I usually do fill them with work, but I would be happier to fill them with people. I am no longer rushing pell-mell from airport to apartment to television studio and back to airport to heaven knows where. These days I look forward to talking with my seatmate on a plane. I greet people in the elevator and even chat with them. I am eager to make the friends I never had time for before. I find myself reaching out more and more.

My grief has also made me more sympathetic and understanding, more sensitive to people. It is like radar. It searches out the grief and pain in other people. I have learned from my own experience how comforting even a few understanding words can be. And how comforting shared tears can be.

Reaching out to people and exercising are two of the most visible changes I have made in my life since Milt died. The swimming pool and exercise room of our apartment house is one of the reasons Milt and I moved there. Sixteen years ago, when I had put on a few too many pounds, I swam them off. It was not easy, but it was enjoyable—and very effective. I eventually worked up to the point where I could swim for an hour, which burned up 600 to 700 calories. Once I reached that goal, I set another for myself. I decided to swim the distance between New York and Princeton, where Lisa was going to college at the time. I marked the fifty-three-mile route on a road map that I tacked up on the wall of my office. Every night when I finished swimming, I charted my progress on the map. And mile by mile I inched down the road map until I reached Princeton. I lost weight and a lot of flab. I went down two dress sizes.

One night this winter I was alone in the apartment feeling lonesome and miserable. I felt I *had* to get out of the apartment. I decided to go down to the swimming pool for the first time in years. I found I was completely out of shape—a couple of laps left me breathless—but when I got upstairs again, I felt wonderful—clean and smooth and rather cheerful. I had not felt that well since Milt's death.

I now try to swim four or five times a week, and I have worked up to being able to swim for an hour again. My new goal is to swim to Davenport, Iowa, where Lisa lives. It is a thousand miles, and it is going to take years. I am still swimming my way through New Jersey, but lap by lap I am on my way. I find having a destination gives me an incentive to swim just one more lap.

I have also started using the machines in the exercise room. I plod along on the treadmill; I row a little; and then I reward myself with a swim.

All this exercise has made a tremendous difference in the way I feel. And in my figure. I mean, it's not perfect, but it could be much worse. It is a lot better than it was six months ago.

Exercise not only makes me feel better physically and emotionally, it makes me feel that I am doing something useful. I am taking care of my body and my health. I am also burning up enough calories so I can eat almost whatever I please without gaining weight.

It has also given me a whole new set of acquaintances, the fitness buffs among my apartment house neighbors. I look forward to seeing them and exchanging a few words. All those years ago when I was "swimming to Princeton," I never said a word to anyone at the pool. I just concentrated on swimming lap after lap after lap, getting it done so I could get back upstairs to Milt. Now I am swimming for the joy of it, and part of that joy is the pleasure I take in my new acquaintances at the pool. Every person you meet, I have discovered, enriches you.

I am also beginning to change the direction of my career. I want to shift the emphasis to public service. Since Milt's death I have become so conscious of all the needs out there—the need for more cancer research, for more hospice programs that allow people to die with minimum pain and maximum dignity, for reversing the pollution of this planet.

I am working to promote research in the field of urology, and particularly bladder cancer, by publicizing the disease and its causes.

Next fall I am going to give a lecture for the Veterans Administration Hospital. This will be the first of the permanent annual Dr. Milton J. Brothers lecture. It pleases me immensely that I was able to establish this.

I am also beginning to speak out against smoking. The statistics on cancer deaths caused by cigarette smoking are appalling. Mark Green, the New York City Commissioner of Consumer Affairs, wrote on the Op Ed page of *The New York Times*, "A thousand times a day or forty times an hour, there is a funeral because someone was addicted to smoking." Milt's was one of those funerals.

If there is anything I can do to prevent another man from dying of bladder cancer caused by cigarette smoking, I am going to do it. Not for Milt—he is dead—but for that other man's wife. No woman should become a widow because of a cigarette.

There is so much that is new in my life that I find myself full of energy. The days fly by. Suddenly I realize I have not cried all week. I realize that I am enjoying life—and then I feel guilty. But not very. There is no reason why I should.

Some call the last stage of grief "acceptance" and define it as the ability to recall one's beloved without pain. But I think it is more than that. You have not worked through the stages of grief until you are ready to plunge into life again. I feel that I am ready, although at times I am still overcome by loneliness and longing. And sometimes I doubt that my life will ever be as good as it was when I shared it with Milt. I have learned, however, that recovery comes in fits and starts, that for every two steps ahead, you fall back one. My life is so much better now than it was eighteen months ago, twelve months ago, six months ago, that I know it will continue to get better. And I will continue to change.

I will always have a pocket of grief in my heart. How could it be otherwise? But that will not keep me from enjoying life. On the contrary, it will make me value every living minute, because now I know how precious each one is.

I am not at all unusual. Most widows discover that there is an end of grief and that life is full of promise again. Sociologist Helena Lopata studied three hundred Chicago widows who lived alone and found that 42 percent of them felt they were freer and more independent than they had been at any time in their lives.

Many had taken up careers, hobbies, or studies they had given up when they got married. Others were active in politics, and some reported that they were just plain having a good time—playing bridge, dancing, traveling, and making new friends. Only 20 percent of the widows she has studied over the years said that they were unhappy.

I know now that I am going to be one of the happy widows. For the first year after Milt died, I was living in the past. Now I am looking to the future. I am walking into tomorrow.

PART
3

~~∾~~

WHAT EVERYONE
SHOULD KNOW
ABOUT GRIEF

Fifteen

It is not only the widow and widower who are beset by grief and suffer the fearful loneliness of loss. Every year, according to the National Academy of Sciences, more than eight million Americans experience the loss of an immediate family member. Parents die. Children die. Brothers and sisters die. Grandparents, aunts and uncles, die. Friends die. Lovers die.

Death steals beloved persons from all of us, but not all losses are from death. The divorcée in her fifties or sixties whose husband has dumped her for a younger woman may grieve as deeply and bitterly as any widow. So may the men and women whose parents or spouses suffer from Alzheimer's or another of the cruel diseases of age that destroy the mind and the personality, leaving only the physical shell—a kind of living death.

I came to realize how little help we extend to these others after giving several lectures on widowhood and the loss of love. I had expected my audiences to be widows like myself. Far from it. There were not only widowers, but middle-aged men and women whose parents had died, people who had lost a good friend, divorcées, and women whose lovers had left them. I found that many of the people in my audiences had been grieving in lonely silence because others did not acknowledge or understand the depth of their grief.

While people condole, for instance, with the man whose mother has died, he is expected to pull himself together and go about his business as usual after the funeral. It does not matter that his grief may be so shattering that he is not able to function normally for months and months. No matter that he is going through the same stages of grief as a widow or widower. No matter that the death of a parent is extremely stressful.

All of us need to become more sensitive to the grief of others. I was not even aware of how deeply my daughter was grieving for her father until several months after his death. In the days immediately after Milt's death, Lisa had been immensely comforting and strong. I don't know how I would have managed without her. But I was so immersed in my own grief that I never gave a thought to how she must be feeling. I knew she was sad and full of tears, but I had no idea how anguished she really felt.

I will always regret that I was so absorbed in my own loss and my own feelings that I did not understand what a blow her father's death had been to my daughter and that I had not tried to comfort her. It had been a one-way street. She gave and I took.

When the time came that we talked with each other about how much we missed Milt, I was startled that she too had gone through periods of anger and intense loneliness. Her feelings duplicated mine in many ways, although her anger was directed somewhat differently.

In the beginning she had felt enormous anger at the way her father had been treated in the hospital. She felt that Milt should have had more personal and more caring treatment—especially since he had been on the staff for so many years and given so much of himself to the hospital.

At one point, she said, she had wanted to bundle him up and take him home to Iowa with her. She was sure that the hospital in Davenport would have been warmer and more caring than the people at Mount Sinai.

She was also angry that no one on the hospital staff had seemed to care about her feelings or mine. No one ever took time to tell us how Milt was doing or what they were planning to try next or even to tell us that he was a good patient. Or that he was very brave—for he was.

Lisa had been surprised by how terribly alone and abandoned she felt after her father died. "After all," she said, "I have Amir. And the four children. Ariel was born just two days before Dad died. It's hard to believe you can feel lonely with a newborn baby in your arms, but I did."

It was easy for me to believe. Lisa had always been Daddy's girl. And she was just like him. She had the same kind of mind, the same personality. There was even a strong physical resemblance. I remember once when she was about six, I met one of my neighbors, and she said, "I just saw Milt skipping down the street wearing a hair ribbon and a little blue coat."

All her life Milt had meant home to Lisa. She did not always know where I was, but Milt was always there. She was welcome to visit his office, and he came home every night. Even though I was careful to leave numbers where I could be reached and I called home every night, it was not the same. She hesitated to call me long distance for help on a home-work assignment or just to chat when she came home from school, because she knew I was busy. Lisa and I were close, but ours was a different rela-tionship from hers with Milt. Milt adored her. He was terribly proud of her, and this gave her a sense of importance and bolstered her self-esteem. He used to tell her that he could always depend on her to do the right thing. She told me that she had always felt secure because he thought she was wonderful.

"I miss talking to Dad so much," she told me. "I still find myself reaching for the telephone to call him—and then I remember. He's not there any longer. It still brings tears to my eyes."

At first, all her memories were painful. But now, more than a year later, the good memories are surfacing, and she takes pleasure in them, although she still feels the loss. Not long ago she told me that she knows what he would say in certain circumstances, and she says it for him. "It makes me feel close to him," she said.

I laughed and hugged her and said, "I do exactly the same thing. I walk into the apartment some nights and I say, 'It's too warm in here,' and I turn down the thermostat."

"But you were always the one who complained that it was too cold," Lisa said.

"I know, but that's what I mean. I always felt cold, but I have changed. Sometimes I feel as if I am turning into your father. Now I say what he would have said."

"I am still lonely," Lisa said. "I think I will always be lonely."

I am sure that she will be. There is no substitute for a father's unconditional love for his daughter. I still miss my own father terribly. There is rarely a day that I do not think of him.

"Even though I am married and have children and my husband loves me dearly, when my father died, I knew there would never again be anyone who loved me the way my father did," a woman told Katherine Donnelly, an authority on bereavement.

"When you lose your parents," said another woman, "you lose someone you can never replace. If your husband dies, you can remarry. If your child dies, you may be able to have another child, but you can only have one father and one mother."

And Jane Brody, the health columnist of *The New York Times*, wrote of her father's death, "Gone was the person who had known me better than anyone else on earth and who had loved and admired me unconditionally since the day I was born."

Nor is there a substitute for a mother's love. A woman's grief over her mother's death, however, is somewhat more complicated. There are many facets to the mother-daughter relationship. Mothers and daughters go through more emotional stages as the daughter grows up than fathers and daughters do. And while a daughter always remains Daddy's little girl, she grows up to be her mother's peer.

One woman told me that she had never really appreciated her mother until she was married and had a child of her own.

"It was two o'clock," she said, "and I had been walking the floor with my colicky four-month-old since midnight, and now I was changing his messy diaper. I was exhausted, ready to cry myself. All of a sudden, I thought, Mom went through all this with me. She must have felt the way I feel now.

"I called her in the morning and told her how much I loved her. She is my best friend as well as my mother."

Very little has been written about the adult child who loses a parent—yet the parent-child relationship is probably the strongest bond that exists, and every year millions of adults lose a parent. Coping with the death of a parent is one of the most important and difficult emotional tasks of adult life.

Professor Andrew Scharlach of the University of Southern California's School of Social Work studied 220 men and women, all of whom had lost one or both parents in the last five years. "Many of them said they felt like orphans," he reported.

Almost half of the group told him that they had had trouble sleeping and coping with day-to-day activities for several months after their mother or father died. More than a third said they thought about their parent often and cried when they did.

A parent's death is also distressing because it is the first intimation of your own mortality. It is like the writing on the wall, and the message is that you, too, will die. "When a parent dies, there is nobody between you and death any longer," explains Professor Scharlach. "Suddenly you're the next generation up."

The death of a parent can affect the adult child's

health, especially a son's. Men are more likely than women to die from accidents, heart disease, cancer, and infectious illnesses after the death of their mother or father. These health hazards are most common during the first year, but the susceptibility to accidents and illness may last as long as six years.

A parent's death also carries a special kind of emotional pain that radiates out into all parts of the adult child's life. "No matter how old a person is," says psychiatrist James Hodge, former chairman of the Department of Psychiatry at Northeastern Ohio University medical school, "a parent's death unleashes a flood of intense emotion. Not just grief, but frequently deep anger." The same kind of anger is experienced by almost every person who has lost a beloved. It is an anger at being abandoned by that person: "How could you leave me!"

This combination of anger and grief is explosive and cannot be repressed indefinitely, says Dr. Hodge. "When the explosion comes, the emotions are often directed at the most convenient target—the husband or wife. And this misdirected anger can drive a wedge into a marriage." The anger may also be directed at someone in the workplace—at a man's employer, for instance, or a rival for promotion—with often unfortunate results.

Guilt may be mixed in with the anger and grief. Most adult children are full of regrets for what they did not say and what they did not do for their parent before his or her death. They wish they had expressed their love and appreciation more. They wish they had not been impatient or critical or had visited their parent more often. All this unfinished business torments them. They think, If only I had done this. . . . If only I had said that. . . ."

This guilt can eat away at the adult child unless he or she comes to terms with it. Some therapists recommend writing a letter to the parent who has died, spelling out how much he or she had meant to you and how you regret that you had not shown your love more often. You may prefer to talk your feelings into a tape recorder. The important thing is to get the feelings out. Once they have been expressed, they are easier to deal with.

People who have tried this approach report that they came to feel they were speaking directly to the parent who had died and that their mother or father understood how they felt. Others have found that once they had listed all the things they regretted, they realized that there was another side to the equation and that they had done many wonderful things for their parents.

Young children suffer more than many people realize from the death of a parent or grandparent, of a sibling or a friend. It is not always easy to be sure how much a child knows or how he feels. Death is not only frightening, it is a concept that small children cannot grasp.

Children should be taught about death. In fact,

without even realizing it, most of us play a game with babies that introduces the idea of death—peek-aboo. Hiding his eyes with his hands and then taking them away, the child dies symbolically for a brief moment and then reassuringly comes alive again. The name *peekaboo*, according to psychologist Ada Maurer, stems from Old English words that mean "dead or alive."

Children's curiosity about death is rarely satisfied. Many parents feel that one should not talk about death with children. The result is that they leave their children to their own fears and speculations, which tend to be far more frightening than the reality. If someone close to a child dies, the child worries that if that person died, so can his parents. And then who will take care of him? If a brother or sister dies, the child is even more frightened. He feels at hazard. Perhaps he will die too, and they will put him in a box and bury him in the ground.

Most children come to accept the knowledge of their own mortality and that of others if their parents are open about the facts of death. If parents talk about death calmly and honestly, the child will learn that death is a part of life.

Toddlers will listen when you tell them that Daddy is dead, and then they will ask, "When is Daddy coming home?" And you explain that Daddy will never be able to come home, because he is dead. The child seems to understand. You may hear her tell a playmate or a neighbor that "Daddy is dead, and he is never going to come home again."

But the next day she will ask, "Why doesn't Daddy want to come home?" It takes a long time, a lot of patience and sensitivity, to help a preschooler grasp the finality of death.

This was exactly the case with my three-year-old granddaughter, Lily.

One afternoon when Lisa and I and Lily were driving to pick up Talya from kindergarten, Lily asked me why Grandpa had died.

I thought fast. I did not want to say he had died because he was old. If I told Lily that her grandpa had died because he was old, then she might worry that I might die. Or her other grandmother. Or her mother. All adults seem old to a three-year-old.

Nor did I want to say that her grandpa died because he was very sick. That can also be terrifying for a child. Any time Mummy or Daddy gets a feverish head cold or an upset stomach, panic can set in. Mummy is sick. Mummy may die. It was just not right for Lily to feel there was a possibility of her parents dying; or even of her remaining grandparents dying.

So I told her, "Grandpa died because he smoked too much."

I felt this was a perfectly safe thing to say. In the first place, it was true. In the second place, since neither her mother nor her father smoked, it would not produce any fears that they might die.

A few weeks later I was happy that I had chosen this explanation. Lisa called to tell me that Lily was going through a very difficult phase. She was waking up at night crying, and she had been having nightmares about bad witches killing people. If I had said that Grandpa had died because he had cancer and was very sick, it would have added one more layer of fear to these preschool fears and have really been hard on her.

Some adults try to skirt the facts of death by telling small children that "Grandpa is sleeping" or "Grandma has gone away for a long visit" or "God loved Daddy so much that He took him up to heaven to be with Him." All these well-intentioned explanations simply add to children's fears. They see their father sleeping and worry that he will disappear just as Grandpa did. Or when Mummy goes to the hospital to have a new baby, they fear that she will never come back. And as for God taking someone up to heaven, that is very scary. He might take Mummy or Daddy, and then what would become of me?

Despite Lily's persistent questions about her grandpa and why he had died, it took her a long time to grasp the concept of death. She used to keep asking when Grandpa was going to come visit. And Lisa kept explaining that Grandpa was dead and he would never come to visit again.

One day Lisa heard her tell her doll, "Grandpa is

dead. He's not going to come to our house anymore."
But five minutes later Lily sought out her mother
and asked, "Can we go see Grandpa at his house?"
It takes a long time for a little girl to grasp the absolute finality of death.

Now that she is three and a half, Lily seems to
have accepted the fact that Grandpa is not going to
return. She is very interested in looking at family
photographs these days and always exclaims delight-
edly, "That's Grandpa!" when she comes across a
picture of Milt. And then she adds dolefully, "Grandpa's dead now."

Talya was five when Milt died. A five-year-old
usually knows that death is final.

Talya seemed to accept Milt's death fairly easily,
but she still misses him. There is a core of sadness
there. Recently when Lisa told her that I was writing
a book about what it feels like to lose someone you
love, she asked Talya, who is now six, "What did it
feel like to you?"

"It made me very sad."

"Why do you think you feel sad?"

"Because I miss him," she said matter-of-factly.

"I miss him, too," Lisa told her. "Tell me, why do
you miss Grandpa? What was special about him?"

Talya thought for a moment, and then she said, "I
miss him because he made me feel very special."

When Lisa told me this, we both cried. He made
us all feel very special.

. . .

The seven- to ten-year-old tends to be full of questions—many of them hard for the surviving parent to deal with, like "Is Daddy cold down there under the ground?" "Does he get wet when it rains?" "Will he turn into a skeleton?" These very specific questions, gruesome as they may seem, are an attempt to absorb the fact of death, to understand it, to make it real. They should be answered straightforwardly and matter-of-factly.

Some people feel, because of these often grisly questions, that the child does not grieve or miss the person who died. He does. One must understand that a child's mourning is an up-and-down thing, whether the youngster is three or thirteen. He may be desperately sad one moment and retreat to his room to be alone; the next moment he is outdoors running and shouting with his friends. This alternation of mourning and joy in life is normal. It is not unthinking, not callous.

I knew my ten-year-old grandson missed his grandfather terribly. They had been very close. Micah had known that Milt was seriously ill. In fact, he had been staying with us one time when I had to rush Milt to the hospital emergency room at five in the morning. Even so, his grandfather's death was a shock. Somehow he had never thought Milt would really die. No one he knew had ever died before.

Lisa had debated about whether or not Micah

should attend his grandfather's funeral. Finally she decided that she did not want to deprive him of his ability to mourn or seem to downplay his grief.

I agreed with Lisa. Most experts are emphatic that it is much harder for children to accept the finality of death if they do not participate in the funeral ceremony and are not taken to visit the cemetery.

She also decided against having the girls attend the funeral. She felt that it would be too much for Lily and Talya to fly to New York from Iowa, sit through the ceremony at the funeral home, be bundled into a car for the drive to the cemetery, and then stand in the January cold for half an hour during the final graveside ceremonies. Again I agreed with her. There was too much traveling and upset involved. They would be too bewildered by the whole thing.

If they had lived closer to the city, I would have advised that they attend the ceremony at the funeral home and, a day or two later, visit his grave at the cemetery. As it was, we took them to visit their grandfather's grave several months later after the unveiling of the tombstone. By then the raw earth had been covered with sod and there was nothing frightening about it.

But Micah was there, both at the funeral home and at the cemetery. Although the funeral was a difficult experience for him, he could see that all of us were overcome with emotion. Surrounded by grieving and weeping relatives and friends of his grandfather, he understood that his own feelings were normal. His grief was very similar to an adult's, but I suspect it was sharper, more poignant than that of most of the mourners, because this was the first death in his life, and the man who died had loved him dearly.

In the months that followed the funeral, Lisa often talked with her son about her father and things they had done together when she was Micah's age. She encouraged him to share his memories of his grandfather. They often cried together as they talked about how much he had meant to them. She thought it important to keep reinforcing the lesson that it was perfectly normal to be sad and to cry.

When I finally got around to packing up Milt's clothes and giving them away, I sent some of his things to Lisa, saying that I thought Micah might like them. There was a leather cap and a woolly scarf that Milt used to wear in the country and some of his books on astronomy.

Lisa and Micah opened the package together. As they unpacked it, Micah began to cry. Lisa told him that it was hard to lose someone you loved very much. She explained that even though you feel pain when a person you love dies, it is important to love people, and that love is the greatest gift you can give anyone. His pain showed how much he had loved his grandfather.

Micah happily wore the leather cap and the scarf all that winter. The books on astronomy are in his bookcase. One of these days I plan to give him Milt's

telescope so he can watch the stars he has been reading about. I know he will treasure it. And perhaps
one day he will give it to his own son. Or grandson.

My grandchildren have now accepted the death of
their grandfather. They have incorporated it into
their lives. They still talk about him and think about
him, but the sadness is evaporating. Soon there will
be nothing left but the happy memories. And that is
the way it should be.

Essentially we are all children. We resist the idea
of death's finality. Grief makes us uncomfortable.
But each and every one of us has lost or will lose a
beloved. We should and can help each other. We can
help by accepting others' tears, by listening to their
memories, to their complaints, their worries, their
anger—just by letting them talk. We can try to soften
their loneliness. In the following two chapters, I suggest ways in which people who have lost a beloved
can help themselves cope with their grief—and how
others can help them.

Sixteen

～✦～

After Milt died, I was at sixes and sevens. I really did not know what to do. The structure of my life had been destroyed. I was fortunate that I have always worked and that the requests for lectures, television appearances, and articles continued. Otherwise I am afraid I might simply have stayed in bed, pulled the covers up over my head, and let the world go by. At least that is what I felt like doing.

Even a psychologist who can identify the stages of her grief and understand her emotions is as miserable as any other woman who has lost her husband. It does not really help to know that loneliness is one of the major components of grief. Every widow discovers that for herself, and she is still as lonely as if she were on an uninhabited planet.

I receive many, many letters saying something along these lines: "My husband died six months ago, and I am so miserable. I do not see how I can go on. Tell me, Dr. Brothers, how do you manage? Can you help me?"

Anyone who is reading this book understands by now that I did not manage my grief any better than any other widow. But I have learned over the past year and a half that there are ways a widow can help herself. I have put together a handful of suggestions for avoiding some of the booby traps widows face and dealing with some of the problems that a woman confronts after her husband's death. Some of them may help you feel a little better—if only momentarily. Some of them may not work for you at all. But if there is anything here that can help you, I will feel grateful.

STAY IN CHARGE OF YOUR OWN LIFE

Do not let others take over your life. Do not let your children or anyone else step in and try to run your life for you. Do not let them manage your money or your activities. Too often relatives, and sometimes friends, tend to think they know how the widow should conduct her life and affairs better than she does herself. This is rarely the case.

You may appreciate it at first when your son or daughter takes over your checkbook and pays your bills and does your income tax for you, but unless you are truly incapacitated, you should thank them after a month or two and say that you now feel ready to deal with these matters. You may not be used to paying bills and balancing a checkbook, but there is nothing all that difficult about these chores. If taxes present a problem, then get an accountant or tax expert to help. If you are over sixty-five, there are free tax preparation services available in most communities run by local senior citizen groups.

Why do I make such a point of this? It is too easy to give up control of your life, to let yourself become your child's child. But you are not a child. You are an adult, and you should be free to make your own decisions, which brings me to another point.

AVOID HASTY DECISIONS

The rule of thumb is that a widow should not make any major decision for at least a year after her husband's death. Obviously this is sometimes impossible. There may be financial considerations that force you to make a decision within weeks of the funeral. In that case try to get the best advice you can.

You will probably find that your adult children, your brother, your brother-in-law, and possibly other members of your family will tell you exactly what you should do. All that is fine. Listen carefully to what they have to say and make notes, but do not rely solely on your family. They are well motivated, but they may not be the best-informed sources on the particular situation.

On a major decision like selling your house, buying a condo, investing the life insurance money, selling stocks, and so on, I strongly advise that you get advice from professionals as well as from your family.

Discuss the impending decision with your attorney, your banker, a trusted friend, and possibly an accountant (if you do not have one, ask your attorney or banker to suggest the name of a reliable person). When you have listened to their advice, think about everything you have learned and then do what you think is best. This is your life, and you should have the ultimate say-so in how you are going to lead it from now on.

But if you can possibly avoid it—do not sell your house, do not move, do not make a major purchase, do not make a major change in your way of life. Put everything on hold for a year.

PLAN FOR THE FUTURE

The elderly widow should take stock of her physical condition and come to a tentative decision about how long she thinks she can continue to live on her own. Your family doctor can help you with this forecast. It is a good idea to see him for a checkup anyway. He will be very frank with you about when and if he thinks it would be wise to change your living conditions. This gives you time to plan.

What about a retirement community? Is a nursing home in your future? Are there any alternatives to this? A live-in companion, perhaps, or a group home? Would you be happy living with one of your children? Would that child be able to give you the care and attention you will need?

The time to think about your choices and to investigate them is now—before you need to make a choice.

MAINTAIN YOUR REGULAR ROUTINE

Many widows are so stunned by their husband's death that they let things slide. Some women report that for months after the funeral they sat in front of the television set for hours on end, barely conscious of what was on the screen. This behavior can lead to acute depression, which can prolong your grief for years and years.

You may feel that there is no point in anything, but push yourself to get up at your usual hour, go to bed at your usual hour, do your shopping, clean your house, and do your other household chores as usual. It is a kind of early therapy for grief. In the early days, when you feel as if your life has disintegrated, the old routine provides a framework that will help you put one foot in front of the other when you think you are too torn apart to even move.

If you vacuum on Mondays and Fridays, play bridge on Wednesdays, and go to the hairdresser Saturday mornings, maintain your schedule until there is a reason to change.

You will make changes eventually, but until you feel a little more in control, stick to the old routine. I learned this bit of wisdom from my mother. When my father died, her life changed drastically from that of an extremely busy attorney who worked five days a week in her husband's law office to that of a lady of leisure.

Fortunately it did not happen quite that fast. It took months to close down the office, busy months of taking care of all kinds of nit-picking details. It was a blessing because it kept her in the old routine of going downtown and working hard all day.

But when the office was finally closed, my mother embarked on a completely different kind of life. She accepted that her life could never be the same again and immediately set about the changeover to a life of leisure. She knew she would not be happy unless she was active, so she geared her activities to fill her days. Instead of shopping once a week, she shopped every day for that day's meals. She could have ordered everything by telephone and had it delivered, but she preferred to go out and choose the five spears of asparagus, the head of lettuce, the lamb chop, and the pint of strawberries that she wanted. She went from the butcher to the baker to the Korean vegetable store, chatting with her neighbors and the storekeepers as she chose her lunch and supper. She also began to play cards every afternoon, something she loves and never had time for when she was working. She is a happy woman, and some of that happiness is due to the routine she worked out for herself.

She settled into this routine very easily, but she admits that it would have been terribly hard for her to switch from one way of life to the other overnight.

PLAN AHEAD FOR ANNIVERSARIES, HOLIDAYS, AND WEEKENDS

Traditional "special" days can be the pits, especially during the first year. The anniversaries are probably the worst. They bring back so many sweet, intimate memories. The holidays were always full of cheer, usually a time of family gatherings where you and your husband were the center. Now you are acutely conscious of his absence, and you may no longer feel you are as important a star in the family constellation as you were when he was alive. The weekends, which were your time to be together, are now empty time.

You cannot turn these days into happy occasions, especially the first year you are alone, but you can make them easier to live through. The secret is planning.

Make a list of the anniversaries and holidays that meant the most to you and then plan how you are going to get through them. The best solution is to surround yourself with people. This helps tremendously. The first Thanksgiving after Milt died, I invited eighteen people to the farm for Thanksgiving weekend. That made nineteen of us for Thanksgiving dinner, and that meant I was much too busy to be miserable. Oh, there were a few tears, but those four days went by in a whirl. There is a great deal to be said for hard work as a means of keeping your mind off yourself.

Widows who do not have family or whose family live too far away to come for holidays should try to spend those days with friends. If that is impossible, spend them with people who might otherwise be alone.

One widow I know has spent the last five Thanksgivings at her church helping to serve turkey dinners for the less fortunate. She is busy all day, helping cook, serving, and cleaning up afterward. "I have no time for tears," she says, "and every year I realize there are many people who are far more alone in this world than I am."

If you know people who are going to be alone on Christmas or Thanksgiving, ask them to have dinner with you. Put together a group of three or four, cook a traditional meal, set a festive table, and do your best to make their holiday a good one. You will find that this will make the day much easier to live through.

Most anniversaries do not lend themselves to being shared with others. I spent the anniversary of Milt's death trying to carry on as usual, but I planned ahead to make it a bit easier. I filled the day with so many appointments that I scarcely had time to draw a breath. I was full of sadness and tears that night when I got home, but I managed to get through the day without wallowing in grief.

Do not make the mistake of trying to escape by going on a cruise during major holidays like Christmas and Thanksgiving or important anniversaries. This may seem like an ideal solution. After all, what could be better than getting away, surrounding yourself with new people, seeing new sights, having new experiences? Well, in fact, nothing could be worse.

Widows have told me they were absolutely miserable on their luxury cruises. They had never felt so lonely in their whole lives. The problem with a cruise is that the passenger list is usually divided into young couples, older couples, and unattached women—widows, divorcées, and single women. This grouping reinforces the widow's feeling of being a second-class citizen. The couples eat with each other; the widow eats alone or with other unattached women. The couples gravitate to other couples during shore excursions; the widow follows along alone or with another widow. At night the couples meet for drinks together and dance together. Although many cruise lines offer free cruises to unattached males in return for their services as dancing partners, the new widow may not feel like dancing. If she does, she knows that her partner is only dancing with her out of duty. A cruise will only make the widow more conscious of what she has lost when she sees couples enjoying themselves.

The time may come in two or three years when you may find a cruise enjoyable, but do not risk it for the first couple of years after your husband's death.

Weekends are hard to cope with because there are so many of them. I tell people to plan a month's worth of weekends at a time. Don't let a Friday night creep up on you and then realize that you are going to be alone for the next two days without a blessed thing to do.

Get out your calendar and write down just how

you plan to spend each Saturday and Sunday for the next month. You may spend Saturday mornings going to the mall, cleaning house, working in the garden, cooking. And Saturday afternoons you may play golf, go for a long walk, spend an hour telephoning friends and family, return your library books. Sunday mornings you may go to church— even if you are not a regular churchgoer, I suggest that you attend services for the first few months after your husband's death, if for no other reason than to be with other people. You may or may not find consolation in the religious message, but one of the best things you can do for yourself is to get out with other people.

One widow volunteered to baby-sit the minister's six-month-old baby on Sunday mornings so his wife could attend services. She gained a double benefit from this. First, she loved babies, and those two hours when she had the baby to herself were pure pleasure. Second, the minister and his wife always brought a few parishioners home to share Sunday dinner with them. And, of course, the widow was always included.

Perhaps you can set apart a couple of hours on Sunday afternoons to write to friends and answer condolence letters. And finish off the weekend by inviting a friend or neighbor for tea or drinks or supper. After that, if you feel like settling down to Sunday-night television, fine.

I don't suggest these activities as a rigid schedule for every widow's weekends, but simply as a stimulus to help you think about how you will fill those days. It takes thought and imagination.

I am not suggesting for one moment that keeping busy is a cure for grief. If only it were that easy! But keeping busy will give you a respite from your grief, and it will keep you involved with the world.

GET OUT OF THE HOUSE

Do anything to get out of the house, even if you do not want to. Get involved in politics, the women's club. Learn how to sign and then volunteer to work with deaf children. Take a first-aid class. Learn word processing. Volunteer at the library, the hospital, the nursing home, the museum. Get a paying job. Find something to do that will get you out of the house at least a couple of days a week.

Widows have a tendency to stay home and cocoon. Do not give in to this inertia. Get yourself up and out. I am not suggesting that you put yourself on a hectic, nonstop schedule, nor am I suggesting that you change your life radically. Not yet, anyway. But I do know that it is better to be up and out than stuck in the house.

I advised against taking a cruise, but getting away for a weekend now and then can do wonders. Just don't go back to the place you and your husband always went and had such a good time. It will make you miserable.

Do something different. Go to Atlantic City and play the slots. Book yourself into a country inn in a scenic spot, where you can go cross-country skiing (you are never too old to learn) or hiking or antiquing and come back and enjoy drinks around the fire at night with the other guests. The Audubon Society has bird-watching weekends. Environmentalists on either coast sponsor weekend whale-watching trips. Spend two days sight-seeing in Boston or New Orleans or San Francisco. A travel agent will have dozens of suggestions in all price ranges. Investigate Elderhostel offerings (check your library for information).

A change of scenery and pace can be very helpful, not only because you are seeing something new, but because you will start to build your own memories, memories of pleasurable days that are not associated with your husband. This is extremely important.

I have such happy memories of Milt that I never want to lose a single one of them. But my life has not stopped. I am still alive. And I want to store up many more happy memories. Creating a new treasury of memories will make your life more fulfilling and make you a more interesting person.

If traveling is out of the question, just getting out of the house for the day helps. Plan a shopping excursion to be followed by a movie. Take your grand-

children to the circus. Think of something you want
to do—and do it.

FIGHT LONELINESS

As soon as you can muster the energy, get together
with your old friends. And work at making new
friends. New friends are important, because widows
find that many old friends, especially those who are
married, tend to drop away. One reason is that they
are couple-oriented, and they do not know how to
deal with an unattached woman. Another reason is
that the younger widow's married friends do not understand what she is going through. They think she
is being too emotional for too long. They get impatient with her grief and start to desert her.

Thus it makes sense to reach out for new friends.
And there is no reason you should not make the first
overtures. If you meet someone who seems pleasant,
suggest going to a movie together or to the bake sale
at the church or out to dinner some night.

Try to talk with one new person a week. You may
not feel like it, but it can be a lifesaver. You may
also find that it is a relief to spend time with someone who does not think of you only as a widow, but
as the kindred soul who loves old Fred Astaire films
or who has a collection of wonderful knitting pat-
terns or knows all about African violets.

I have written about how my life, combining an

often hectic career with marriage and family, allowed me no time for friends. I never anticipated how much I would miss the friends I never made until my husband died. In the course of my work I have met hundreds and hundreds of people all across the country. Now I have started trying to turn some of these acquaintances into friends. I know they will enrich my life.

The number of widow groups has increased tremendously over the past few years. Many women find them of enormous help. One of the great advantages of these groups is that you are not seen as "poor Millie" whose husband has died and who is now all alone in the world and full of grief. In a widow group you are seen as that "really sensible Millie" whose husband has died and who is now reaching out for help with the problems confronting her. There is an enormous difference. And it can be extremely helpful to learn how other women dealt with some of the problems you are facing. You will find that you can talk to other widows as you cannot talk to friends or relatives. These women know what you are going through. They have been there. Don't deprive yourself of this source of comfort and support.

Your church or temple and the American Association of Retired Persons and other agencies can put you in touch with one of these groups. Some put notices of their meetings in local newspapers. You should have no problem finding a group. I never became part of one for the reasons that I explained in chapter 11, but I am sure I would have found the association helpful.

BE GOOD TO YOURSELF

If a woman ever needed coddling, a widow is that woman. The person who loved and cherished you has gone, but there is no reason you should not cherish yourself.

You may not feel like paying much attention to your looks, but get yourself to the hairdresser. Just having someone fuss over you will help. And if you have always wanted to color your hair, this is the time. You will be surprised at the lift it will give you. I belong to the "forever blond" school, but hair colorings today are so subtle and so safe that you will find you have literally dozens of shades to choose from. One nice thing if your hair is beginning to thin: hair color gives your hair more body.

I am all for hands-on therapy. When there is no one at home to give you a hug or rub your back or knead that kink out of your shoulder, I believe in finding a substitute. Make an appointment for a facial, for a massage. They are wonderfully pampering, and they are good for you. They stimulate your circulation, help you relax—and make you feel and look better. Neither a massage nor a facial will erase your grief, but they will give you an hour's respite from it.

EXERCISE

Physical exercise is one of the most positive things you can do for yourself. I guarantee that it will make you feel a little better—at least for the moment. And that is all one can expect in the early months of grief.

The secret of benefiting from exercise is to find something you enjoy and then do it regularly. How do you find an exercise you will enjoy?

Borrow exercise videos from the library or rent them from a video store until you find one that suits you. And then buy that one.

Check out your local YWCA or YMCA. They have exercise classes geared to all ages and fitness levels. Y's also have swimming pools, and if your swimming never got beyond a dog paddle, they have swimming classes. I have found swimming a wonderful exercise as well as an energy booster (see chapter 14 for more about this).

While you are at the Y, ask about their exercise machines. There is bound to be something that will appeal to you. One widow swears by her cross-country skiing machine. She used it at the Y and liked it so much that she bought one, which she keeps in her bedroom. "When I'm down and weepy and miserable," she told me, "I get on it for fifteen or twenty minutes, and I always feel better for it. Just moving my body seems to make life appear more manageable."

There are also many independent exercise classes. Check the Yellow Pages to see what is available in your area. Most of these offer a free trial class. Those that don't usually permit you to observe a class or two.

If you prefer, you may simply devise your own exercise schedule. One woman in my apartment house walks four miles a day five days a week. She started out walking one mile a day every other day. "I love it," she says. "There's always something different to look at, a different route to take. I have a waterproof outfit, and I even walk in the rain."

Dr. Karl Menninger of the famous Menninger Clinic always used to say, "Exercise is of definite relief to most depressed people. Plain hard work will serve equally well."

MASTURBATE

I am quite serious. Most widows' sexual drive shuts down completely after their husband's death. I know mine did for months and months and months. But there comes a time when it revives. Then what do you do?

There is an easy and natural answer—masturbate.

It is a release and a comfort. It takes care of that part of your life. Think of it as a crutch that allows you not to feel like a needy, sexually deprived person.

Physiologically it is good for you because it keeps the tissues moist. And if someday there is a special man in your life again, you will be able tc enjoy sex more than if you allowed your vaginal tissues to wither away.

Masturbation does not take the place of your husband in any way. In fact, it is impossible to think about him when you masturbate, because the thought that he is not with you is too painful. Pain and sex are incompatible. So you fantasize, and that permits you an additional escape.

Some women are embarrassed about masturbating, but there is no reason to be. It is a very natural thing, and it leaves you better off. There is no reason you should not use this release.

CRY IF YOU WANT

Do not feel that you must repress your tears. Crying helps (see chapter 8 for an explanation of the benefits of tears). And do not let other people stop you. The natural tendency is to say, "Now, now, don't cry. You'll make yourself sick." This is nonsense. You cannot feel worse than you feel now. Others want you to stop crying because your tears make them uncomfortable. There is not much you can do about their discomfort, but do not let them make you feel that crying is bad for you. It is not.

BEWARE OF PILLS AND ALCOHOL

These may seem to offer an escape or to blunt the edge of grief, but this is a temporary illusion. I do not mean that you should not a have a glass of wine or a Scotch or whatever, but extreme moderation is called for. You are under a terrible stress. Do not make it worse.

As for tranquilizers and sleeping pills, follow your doctor's advice. These can become addictive. The last thing you need is to develop a chemical dependency.

If you even suspect you are drinking too much or taking too many pills, see your doctor immediately and ask for his or her help.

CHECK YOUR PROGRESS

Take time every three months to think back and assess your progress. Do you feel a little better than you did three months ago? Or worse? Are you eating better? Are you coping with everyday life more easily? Are you crying less? Or more? Do you feel less depressed? Or more?

You must not expect that your answers will all be positive. In any three-month period you may feel that everything is worse than it was before. But as the months go by you will notice small signs of improvement. It was more than six months before I realized that I actually did feel a little more together than I had during the first six weeks.

Each widow has her own timetable of grief. These three-month checks will help you measure your progress. And if, after a year, you feel that you have made no significant progress in any area, it might be wise to consult your doctor or therapist. They can both help and reassure you.

Don't expect that your grief will be history in a year. Some women seem to be able to grieve very efficiently and are able to get on with their lives in a matter of months, but others may need two or three years or even more (researchers have found that some people need six years) before they have worked through their grief. You will adjust to your changed life eventually. It may be impossible to believe this during the first months after your husband's death, but it is true.

Every widow must make her own way. Yours may be quite different from mine. Listen to your inner self. You know what is right for you better than anyone else.

Seventeen

⟋⟍

Friends and relatives of the bereaved are full of love and sorrow. They want to help, but their help is sometimes misguided. Too often they think in terms of "ought" and "should." There is little help in these concepts, and less comfort. Some of the things people say and do with the best of intentions only make the widow feel worse. The suggestions that follow are intended as a guide for those who truly want to comfort and help.

WRITE TO HER

I received an avalanche of letters after Milt's obituary appeared in *The New York Times*. The post

243

office sent them around by the mailbag. Most of them were wonderful, and although they did not lessen my grief, they did comfort me—especially letters from people who had been Milt's friends or patients. I never tired of reading their praises.

Some excerpts:

"Milton loved everyone. . . . How he loved life . . . and people, characters . . . everyone. He brought a special kind of happiness to everyone. I'm so sad, but I can hear Milton advising me that life goes on and to laugh it up, as he always did."

"I for one shall not think of his recent illness and suffering, but of all the years we shared from our youth on. God knows we were silly and had laughs galore. I treasure the role he played in my life. As the rabbi so aptly said, 'It's not the birth or the death, but the path between where we leave our mark.' I am so pleased to have walked part of that path with Milt."

"I feel that, in a way, Milt will live on here in Wingdale [where the farm is]—where he seemed to be so close to the earth and stars."

"My husband and I and several other family members were patients of your late husband. He was a wonderful doctor and a very special person. He had a way of always making us feel better, emotionally if he could not physically. He knew that sometimes uplifting people's spirits was the best medicine. There are very few physicians like him, and we miss him very much."

"Milt was my friend, and was a very important part of my life during those tough years after coming out of the service and readjusting to being a freshman at Cornell. I remember the struggles he went through to gain admission to medical school and how well he did later in establishing a prestigious practice and how he became respected in his selected field of specialization. I remember his kindness to me as a patient.

"My loss is very deep, as I know yours is. But if one has to die young, and Milt certainly went before his time, then at least one can have the satisfaction of leaving behind a life dedicated to his profession and his patients, in which he lived every single minute to its fullest."

Condolence letters are not easy to write—or read. I cried when I read letters like those I have quoted, but at the same time I was so pleased that people remembered Milt as he was—such a good man, dedicated doctor, and loving friend.

And then there were letters from other widows who wrote to share their experiences with me. I found those comforting, even though they too provoked tears. Their stories were so similar to mine, filled with so many parallels. They made me understand that I was not the only person going through this terrible experience, and they helped immeasurably.

Letters like this one:

"Greg used to say to me, 'If I died, what would you miss most?' I'd answer things like his laugh or his smile, but not until he was gone did I realize the only thing I missed nonstop was his physical presence—the person to laugh with, share with, bounce ideas off of and get advice, even his encouragement on my cooking or how I looked or what I had accomplished."

And this one:

"My husband, like yours, died of cancer. He was only sixty-three, and he should have lived another twenty years. I was almost paralyzed by my grief for months and months. I cried when I woke up in the morning. I cried when I went to bed at night. I could not take pleasure in anything. A beautiful sunset? So what. My neighbor brought me fresh vegetables from her garden. So what. My daughter cleaned my house every week for the first six months, because I just could not summon the energy to do it myself.

"But now, after three years, I am well over the worst. I am full of energy again. I enjoy life. I went back to work a year ago after thirty-five years as a housewife, and I love it.

"I'm writing to reassure you that you too will recover and find life good again. I know this will sound impossible to you right now, but believe me, you will."

There was one letter that especially meant a lot to me, simply because the writer had remembered me. "I was really touched and deeply moved while watching you on television this morning," she wrote. "I did not see Dr. Joyce Brothers, but Joyce Diane Bauer from Far Rockaway High School, shy, sweet, and so vulnerable. This note is to let you know many people are sharing your grief."

Condolence letters can help a widow tremendously if they offer encouragement or share memories. I have gone back repeatedly for comfort or inspiration to some of the letters I received. I have kept many of the letters about Milt for my grandchildren. When they are older, I will share these letters with them so they will know how much others thought of their grandfather.

FOLLOW THE GOLDEN RULE OF COMFORTING

Try to put yourself in the widow's place. It is almost impossible to sense exactly how devastated and lost she is. You may get an approximate idea of how she feels from asking yourself the questions in "the widow game" that I described in the first chapter. Once you have done this, if you will follow the biblical injunction, "Do unto others as you would be done by," I am sure that you will be able to comfort and console her.

AVOID THE IMPOSSIBLE QUESTION

The impossible question is the most natural and caring question. It takes the form of "How are you?" or "How are you doing?" or "How are you bearing up?" It is impossible to answer. If she tells the truth and says, "Rotten . . . terrible . . . I wish I were dead," most people do not know where to go from there.

The widow knows what you want her to say: "Oh, I'm doing pretty well," or, "Not too bad," or, "I'm managing." She knows that you want her to reassure you, so you will not feel as uncomfortable as you would if faced with her raw misery.

What do you say instead?

Say, "I've been thinking about you a lot. Would it be all right if I dropped by this afternoon? I really want to see you." And when you drop by, bring her a small steak or your famous meat loaf or a pint of her favorite ice cream.

Ask, "Is there something I can do for you? . . ." Do you need to be driven anywhere? . . ." "Can I take the children for the afternoon? . . ." "John wants to go over to your place tomorrow and mow the lawn. Is that all right with you?"

And if you really want to know how she is, ask, "Have you been getting any sleep?" She probably has not been sleeping well. It is easier for her to answer this kind of question, which indicates a real desire to know how she is, than a general question like "How are you doing?"

ENCOURAGE HER TO TALK

Most widows crave opportunities to talk about their beloved. Listening is one of the best things you can do to help. She needs to talk about her loss. She may want to talk about his last illness or how he died or how extremely lonely and disoriented she feels and how hopeless everything seems.

Such talk may make you acutely uncomfortable. You may feel that she should not dwell on such subjects, that she is being morbid, that she should make an effort to put all that behind her.

And that is exactly what she is trying to do. By talking about what happened, about the details of his illness and/or the circumstances of his death, by incessantly going over her memories, she is little by little putting an end to what have been the most important years of her life. This is normal and healthy. She should not be discouraged from doing this.

Years ago a Washington journalist who covered the assassination of President John F. Kennedy told me of how shocked he had been when Mrs. Kennedy, in her blood-spattered skirt, got off the plane and started telling everyone over and over just what had happened in that car in the motorcade. I told him I saw nothing shocking about it. Psychologically it was the best thing she could have done. That horror had to be talked about and faced.

When I spoke to a group of widows and widowers recently, I advised them to be open about their feelings and let their relatives and friends know how painful their grief was. I explained that talking about how they felt would help.

A man interrupted from the audience, saying, "But no one wants to listen."

A woman chimed in, "My brother told me to snap out of it. He said everyone would think I was crazy if I kept on talking about him and crying. He said Norman had been dead for ten months and it was time for me to turn off the waterworks."

I told my audience that grief, and especially tears, makes some people so uncomfortable that they try to make you repress your feelings and that they do not realize how cruel and thoughtless they are being.

Time does not heal grief. People handle their grief in their own individual ways. For relatives and friends to expect a widow to conform to their time schedule of mourning is unrealistic.

LET HER CRY

Nor should anyone demand that a woman "turn off the waterworks." Just as a sensitive listener helps a woman come to terms with her grief, so do her tears.

They may make you uncomfortable. You may want her to stop crying, but this means you are putting your own feelings ahead of hers. Let her cry. Tears are a kind of first aid for grief.

John James, founder of the Grief Recovery Institute of Los Angeles, tells a story of a telephone conversation that made me shiver with sympathy and horror. He could barely hear the woman on the other end of the line. "I don't want my son to hear me," she explained when he asked her to speak up. Her husband had died a year ago. Her son and his wife had come to spend the first anniversary of his death with her.

"They keep telling me that I should be fine now, that it's been a year since he died, that I should not be crying anymore."

"That's nonsense," said John James. "You cry because you need to cry." He helped her work out a sentence to use during her son's visit whenever she felt it was needed. "When I cry, I don't need to be fixed, because there is nothing wrong with me."

So when the widow cries, just push the box of tissues over to her and be patient.

STICK WITH HER

The loneliness is the worst part of grief. At least I found it so. I was fortunate in having a daughter, a mother, a sister, and a sister-in-law who were there for me as much as they could be.

I discovered that I was very fortunate. Researchers have found that the majority of families don't really stay involved with the widow very long after the funeral.

Almost two-thirds of the widows in one study reported that their husband's relatives had not even helped with the funeral arrangements. Less than a quarter had been visited by their in-laws after the funeral. Half of the widows said that their children had no contact at all with their dead father's family.

It is not only the in-laws who drop away. The widow's own family and grown children, although they are usually available for emergencies, see less and less of her as the months go by.

This behavior is unfortunate, because other studies show that a widow seems to work through her grief sooner and more successfully when her family and friends are supportive and understanding.

It is important to realize that the widow needs you—even if she acts as though she does not. Stay in touch with her. It is not better to leave her alone to "work it out." She will be alone too much as it is. Keep asking her to supper or whatever. She may refuse time after time after time. But the time will come when she will want to say yes. And if you do not keep calling, she will be too embarrassed to call you and say, "Do you still want to see me?" So stay with it. Keep calling her to see how she is and ask her to have supper with you. One day she will say yes.

SHOW YOUR LOVE

A widow is touch needy. Suddenly there is no one to cuddle up to in bed, no one to sit with shoulder to shoulder while watching television, no one to pat her on the bottom.

A hug can be immensely comforting. So is having one's hand held or a pat on the shoulder or a kiss on the cheek. Warning: Do not take this as permission to come on to the widow sexually.

REFRAIN FROM GIVING ADVICE

Do not tell the widow that she should sell the house and buy a condo or move to an apartment or get rid of the car or eat better balanced meals or put the insurance money into mutual funds. These may be very good suggestions, but giving advice—unless it is asked for—is intrusive, annoying, and arrogant.

But what if she asks for advice? That is something

else again. In that case give her the very best and considered advice that you can come up with. But— and this is important—do not feel angry with her or upset if she does not follow your advice. She may, and should, have asked several people for advice on the same subject. Whatever course of action she decided upon, be assured that your advice helped clarify her thinking.

And next time she asks for advice, give her the best advice you can again. Do not get huffy and say, "Last time I gave you advice, you paid no attention to it." Perhaps you do feel a bit miffed that she did not take your advice, but do you always take the advice you are given when you ask for it? Don't let your ego get in the way of helping her.

Epilogue

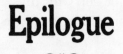

Am I cured and whole again? Has Milt become part of the past? Ah, no. He is always with me, will always be with me. But I have done with the worst of my grieving—or almost. The truth is that my grief is for myself, for my loss.

How could I grieve for Milt? Looking back now, I would not have had him live one hour longer, one minute longer, one second. How could I wish that his suffering be prolonged? How cruel that would have been!

He was a good man. He had a good life. The world is better for his having lived. I have made my peace with his death, but his loss will always be my loss, a part of my life, a part of myself that was ripped out of me.

And if there should ever be another good man with whom I share my life, there will still be that empty corner of my soul. I know what I had and what I lost. I hope I will not spend the rest of my life alone. But if I do, I will not be sorry for myself.

Life goes on, and I am ready to join the parade again.